W9-CCS-185

ERRATUM

The Author
P. 151, last line, "file" should read "life"

HEARTBREAK HOUSE

Preludes of Apocalypse

TWAYNE'S MASTERWORK STUDIES

Robert Lecker, General Editor

HEARTBREAK HOUSE

Preludes of Apocalypse

A. M. Gibbs

TWAYNE PUBLISHERS • NEW YORK
Maxwell Macmillan Canada • Toronto
Maxwell Macmillan International • New York Oxford Singapore Sydney

822.912
Shaw

Twayne's Masterwork Studies No. 136

Heartbreak House: Preludes of Apocalypse
A. M. Gibbs

Copyright © 1994 by Twayne Publishers

Twayne Publishers
Macmillan Publishing Company
866 Third Avenue
New York, New York 10022

Maxwell Macmillan Canada, Inc.
1200 Eglinton Avenue East
Suite 200
Don Mills, Ontario M3C 3N1

Library of Congress Cataloging-in-Publication Data
Gibbs, A. M. (Anthony Matthews), 1935–
  Heartbreak house : Preludes of apocalypse / A. M. Gibbs.
    p. cm.—(Twayne's masterwork studies ; 136)
  Includes bibliographical references and index.
  ISBN 0-8057-8099-8 — ISBN 0-8057-4454-1 (pbk.)
  1. Shaw, Bernard, 1856–1950. Heartbreak House. I. Title. II. Series.
PR5363.H43G53 1994
822'.912—dc20   93-44857
                                                                             CIP

The paper used in this publication meets the minimum requirements of American National Standard for Information Sciences—Permanence of Paper for Printed Library Materials. ANSI Z39.48-1984.∞ ™

10 9 8 7 6 5 4 3 2 1 (alk. paper)

10 9 8 7 6 5 4 3 2 1 (pbk.: alk. paper)

Printed in the United States of America.

SSB

To Donna

Contents

Illustrations

Bernard Shaw at age 60.
Photograph courtesy of the British Library. Used by permission.

Note on the References and Acknowledgments

All in-text quotations from *Heartbreak House* are from *The Bodley Head Bernard Shaw: Collected Plays with Their Prefaces*, volume 5, edited by Dan H. Laurence (London, Sydney, and Toronto: Max Reinhardt, The Bodley Head, 1972). Quotations from Shaw's other plays are also from this seven-volume edition: the volume and page numbers are cited parenthetically in the text.

I am glad to acknowledge here the assistance and advice of many people who have contributed to the preparation of this book. During the early stages of research I was greatly helped by Mrs. Juliet McLean, who carried out an extensive survey and analysis of secondary materials relating to *Heartbreak House*. This survey was further added to by Ms. Marcelle Freiman. Dr. Penny van Toorn's work on another project, a chronology of Shaw's life and career, has also been of assistance in the writing of this book. During my final stages of writing, Dr. Sue Kossew and Dr. Geoff Windon made most helpful suggestions about the text and patiently endured and amended my aberrations from the publisher's style sheet. For their help and advice, thanks are also due to Professor Robert Lecker, General Editor, Masterwork Studies, and Barbara Sutton of Twayne Publishers. My wife, Donna, generously spared time from her own work to read and comment creatively on the book as it developed.

I wish also to thank the staff of the following institutions for their kind assistance: the Billy Rose Theater Collection, Lincoln Center, and the New York Public Library; the Birmingham Shakespeare Institute; the British Library Department of Manuscripts and Reading Room; the Dennis Wolanski Library, Sydney Opera House; the Fisher Library, University of Sydney; the Hofstra University Library; the *Punch* Library; the Macquarie University Library; the Melbourne Theatre Company; the Theatre Museum, Covent Garden; and the Victoria and Albert Museum.

Permission to quote from the works and correspondence of Shaw has been kindly granted by The Society of Authors, on behalf of the Bernard Shaw Estate.

Research for the book was carried out with the aid of grants from the Australian Research Council and Macquarie University.

Chronology: Bernard Shaw's Life and Works

1856	George Bernard Shaw born 26 July in Dublin, the third child of George Carr Shaw, a sometimes amiable but weak and unsuccessful corn merchant, and Lucinda Elizabeth Shaw, a talented singer.
1866–1873	The Shaw family shares a house with an eccentric Dublin conductor (George Vandeleur Lee), with whom Lucinda Shaw collaborates in presenting amateur concerts and operas.
1867	Shaw enters the Wesleyan Connexional, the first of several schools he disliked, preferring what he called the three colleges of his "university": the National Gallery of Ireland, Lee's Amateur Musical Society, and a summer cottage at Dalkey Hill, outside Dublin.
1871	Leaves school and becomes a clerk, and later cashier, in a Dublin land agent's office.
1873	Lucinda Shaw, accompanied by her younger daughter, Agnes, leaves Dublin for London where she practices as a music teacher. Her elder daughter, Lucy, joins them later.
1876	Shaw moves to London after the death of his sister Agnes to live with his mother and Lucy.
1877–1883	Writes five novels and some music criticism; develops interest in socialism.
1881	Begins a flirtation with Alice Lockett, the first of his numerous love affairs.
1884	Joins the Fabian Society and subsequently becomes one of its leading figures.
1885	Surrenders his virginity to a passionate widow, Jenny Patterson.
1888	Reviews music for *The Star* under the pen name Corno di Bassetto until 1890.

1889	Is sent a review copy of Madame Blavatsky's *The Secret Doctrine*, which he forwards to Annie Besant, who becomes a convert to Theosophy. Attends performance of Henrik Ibsen's *A Doll's House*.
1890	Becomes music critic to *The World*, using his own name.
1891	Ibsen's *Ghosts* performed at Royalty Theatre, London. Shaw's study, *The Quintessence of Ibsenism*, published.
1892	First full-length play, *Widowers' Houses*, performed, closing after only two performances. Shaw speaks on woman suffrage in London.
1893	Attends performance of Arthur Wing Pinero's play *The Second Mrs. Tanqueray*, in which Mrs. Patrick (Stella) Campbell plays the female lead. William Gladstone's Liberal government sets aside Fabian-inspired reforms.
1894	*Arms and the Man* performed in London.
1895–1898	Becomes drama critic for the *Saturday Review* and wages war on the nineteenth-century theater.
1896	Travels to Paris to see Ibsen's *Peer Gynt*.
1898	Seven early plays published under the title *Plays Pleasant and Unpleasant*. Marries Charlotte Payne-Townshend.
1899	*You Never Can Tell* presented by the Stage Society. Boer War begins.
1900	*Candida* presented by the Stage Society.
1901	Queen Victoria dies; Edward VII becomes king.
1902	Boer War ends.
1901–1903	Composition and publication of *Man and Superman: A Comedy and a Philosophy*, embodying Shaw's "new religion" of Creative Evolution.
1903	Emmeline Pankhurst forms the Women's Social and Political Union (WSPU) to agitate for women's rights.
1904–1907	Shaw is leading playwright in the Granville Barker and J. E. Vedrenne productions at the Court Theatre. New Shaw plays include *John Bull's Other Island, Major Barbara*, and *The Doctor's Dilemma*.
1905	Einstein propounds his Special Theory of Relativity.
1906	Liberal government returned in general election. Twenty-nine Labour members of Parliament are also elected, a watershed in British political representation.
1908	*Getting Married* presented at the Haymarket Theatre. Shaw

	participates in huge demonstration (estimated at between 250,000 and 500,000) for woman suffrage in Hyde Park, London. Visits August Strindberg in Stockholm.
1910	Edward VII dies; George V becomes king. Postimpressionist exhibition held in London. E. M. Forster's *Howards End* published. *Misalliance* presented at the Duke of York Theatre.
1911	*Fanny's First Play* runs for more than 200 performances. Port of London dockers strike in support of a basic minimum wage. Shaw attends production of Anton Chekhov's *The Cherry Orchard* in London. First London production of Strindberg's *The Father*.
1912	Shaw begins affair with Stella Campbell (model for Eliza Doolittle and Hesione Hushabye). Begins writing *Pygmalion*. First performance of Strindberg's *Miss Julie* in London, in a translation partly by Shaw's sister Lucy. Strindberg's *Creditors* also presented in London. The *Titanic* sinks.
1913	*Androcles and the Lion* presented at St. James's Theatre. Lucinda Shaw dies. Shaw speaks in support of the striking Irish transport workers.
1914	Eliza's use of word "bloody" as an intensive causes a sensation in first London production of *Pygmalion*. World War I begins, forestalling planned general strike. Lord Grey remarks, "The lamps are going out all over Europe; we shall not see them lit again in our lifetime." Women supporting the war distribute white feathers in the street to young men not in uniform. Shaw writes controversial pamphlet "Common Sense about the War" and attracts much hostility. Ivor Novello composes the patriotic song "Keep the Home Fires Burning (Till the Boys Come Home)."
1915	Battles of Loos and Ypres; landings at Gallipoli. Coalition government formed under Herbert Henry Asquith. Shaw is expelled from Dramatists' Club because of his attitude toward the war.
1916	Battles of Verdun and the Somme. Lloyd George becomes prime minister, appointing Lord Devonport (one of Shaw's models for Boss Mangan) as Food Controller, a post he holds till 1917. Easter Rising in Dublin. Shaw witnesses the shooting down of a zeppelin near his home in October.
1916–1917	Starts writing *Heartbreak House* in March, calling the play "Lena's Father" and then "The Studio in the Clouds"; finally settles on *Heartbreak House* in May 1917.

1917	Bolsheviks take control in the Russian Revolution. United States enters the war. Food rationing introduced in Britain. Shaw visits the front lines in France and Belgium at the invitation of Sir Douglas Haig.
1918	Stella Campbell's son, Beo, is killed in the war. The vote is granted to British women over the age of 30.
1919	Treaty of Versailles signed. *Heartbreak House* published. Lady Astor becomes first woman member of Parliament.
1920	*Heartbreak House* has its world premiere at the Garrick Theater in New York on 10 November (runs for 125 performances). League of Nations formed. Civil War in Ireland. D. H. Lawrence's *Women in Love* published.
1921	First British production of *Heartbreak House* staged at the Royal Court Theatre on 18 October (runs for 63 performances). Irish Free State established. W. B. Yeats's *Michael Robartes and the Dancer* published; includes "The Second Coming."
1922	Shaw's five-play cycle, *Back to Methuselah*, presented in New York. T. S. Eliot's *The Waste Land* published. Stella Campbell publishes her autobiography, which includes some of Shaw's letters.
1923	*Saint Joan* staged in New York. Stanley Baldwin becomes British prime minister. D. H. Lawrence's *Kangaroo* published.
1924	First London production of *Saint Joan*.
1925	First public performance in England of the previously banned *Mrs. Warren's Profession*.
1926	Shaw receives 1925 Nobel Prize for Literature, joking that it was awarded "as a token of gratitude for a sense of world relief"—since he had published nothing in 1925. General strike in May. Television is demonstrated for the first time by J. L. Baird.
1928	*The Intelligent Woman's Guide to Socialism* published. Votes given to women as fully as to men. First "talkie" (sound) films shown.
1929	*The Apple Cart* presented at the first Malvern Festival. Labour government returned under Ramsay Macdonald. New York stock market collapses.
1931	Shaw visits Russia (with Conservative MP Lady Astor) and meets Joseph Stalin.
1932	Writes the prose fable *The Adventures of the Black Girl in Her*

Search for God during a visit to South Africa. First production of *Too True to Be Good*. Hunger march of unemployed to London.

1933   *On the Rocks* performed at the Wintergarden Theatre, London. Adolf Hitler becomes German chancellor. The Shaws go on a round-the-world cruise.

1935   *The Simpleton of the Unexpected Isles* presented at Malvern. Italy invades Abyssinia.

1936   *The Millionairess* presented in Vienna. George V dies; Edward VIII becomes king and then abdicates; George VI becomes king. Spanish Civil War begins.

1938   *Geneva*, a play lampooning fascist leaders of the 1930s (Hitler, Francisco Franco, Benito Mussolini), is presented at Malvern. Shaw composes film scenario for *Pygmalion*. Britain, France, Germany, and Italy sign Munich Agreement, intended to appease Hitler, which clears the way for the dismemberment of Czechoslovakia.

1939   Hitler annexes Austria and orders invasion of Poland. Britain declares war on Germany.

1940   Shaw composes material for film version of *Major Barbara*. Stella Campbell dies. Winston Churchill becomes prime minister.

1943   Charlotte Shaw dies. Shaw completes the sociopolitical treatise *Everybody's Political What's What*.

1945   Cooperates with Gabriel Pascal in the filming of *Major Barbara*. Germany surrenders. Labour wins election under Clement Atlee, defeating Churchill's Conservative party. United States drops atomic bomb on Hiroshima on 6 August.

1946   Shaw celebrates his ninetieth birthday.

1949   Writes a puppet play, *Shakes versus Shav*, featuring a tableau from *Heartbreak House*. *Buoyant Billions* presented at the revived Malvern Festival.

1950   Shaw dies at age 94 on 2 November: there are front-page media reports of his death around the world; the lights are dimmed in salute on Broadway.

LITERARY AND HISTORICAL CONTEXT

1

Revolution and Struggle:
The Theatrical and Historical Milieux

When Bernard Shaw arrived in London from Dublin in 1876 a revolution in the history of world drama was about to take place in another country. The following year there appeared the first of the 12 plays about contemporary life and society by the Norwegian playwright Henrik Ibsen. These plays transformed the ways in which human psychology, personal and sexual relations, social institutions, and value systems were explored and presented onstage. By the end of the following decade Ibsen had begun to make a profound impact on English theatrical and intellectual life, and Bernard Shaw had trumpeted Ibsen's achievement with a lengthy lecture to the Fabian Society that was published in 1890 as *The Quintessence of Ibsenism*.

In the meantime, another towering figure, the Swedish dramatist August Strindberg, had begun to emerge as a leader in the late-nineteeth-century revolution in dramatic values. Strindberg's reputation took longer to spread to England, but by 1908 Shaw had met the eccentric Swedish genius and was certainly well familiar with his plays. In some respects Strindberg's drama directly contrasts with Ibsen's, most markedly in *The Father* (1887), which presents an angry retort from the male viewpoint to Ibsen's treatment of the relations between the sexes in *A Doll's House*. In *The Father*, as in *Heartbreak House*, the female dominates the male and reduces him to infantile subservience. (The Father ends up dying in a straitjacket, "lovingly" fitted onto him by his Old Nurse). But however differently they may have viewed the relations between the sexes in their plays, Ibsen and Strindberg had in common the fact that their works show an extraordinary degree of candor and realism in the way in which sexual relations and social institutions could be treated as dramatic material. "I . . . find the joy of life in its strong and cruel struggles," wrote Strindberg in the Preface to one of his plays.[1]

Ibsen's and Strindberg's creative grappling with life's "strong and cruel struggles," such as that between Nora and Torvald at the end of *A Doll's House*, the Captain and Laura in *The Father*, or the Daughter of Indra and the Lawyer in Strindberg's *The Dream Play* (1904), injected new life into the nineteenth-century dramatic tradition and helped to create a new theatrical environment in which the depths of human relations could be plumbed, and previously unsayable things said. Shaw's *Heartbreak House*, along with his other plays of cruel but comic candor, such as *Misalliance* (1909), can be seen as products of this new environment.

Shaw was a champion of the avant-garde in late–nineteenth-century drama. He was also very familiar from his boyhood with the older popular traditions of the theater of his day. In his study *Shaw and the Nineteenth-Century Theater* (1963) Martin Meisel has shown the pervasive influence on Shaw's own plays of popular nineteenth-century forms such as the farce, the melodrama, the pantomime, historical romance, military adventure, religious drama, and extravaganza. Even in such a highly sophisticated play as *Heartbreak House* there are vestiges of nineteenth-century stereotypes, as Meisel argues: "Ellie Dunn, the Ingenue, Hector Hushabye, the Romantic Lead, Boss Mangan, the ominous Heavy, Captain Shotover the eccentric Old Man . . . Hesione and Ariadne, Heavy Heroine and somewhat sophisticated Soubrette.[2]

This list suggests a greater degree of stability in the characterization than Shaw's play shows. Ellie, for example, does not remain an ingenue (Shaw in fact described her as the "heavy lead" of the play),[3] and the haughty Lady Utterword can only just be squeezed into the category of pert comic maidservant! Nevertheless, the ghosts of several nineteenth-century character stereotypes are clearly present as part of the multifaceted selves of the characters Shaw has created, and there are also clear reminiscences of nineteenth-century farce in *Heartbreak House*.

Shaw's experience of "the old drama and the new" (to borrow the title of a book by his friend and first English translator of Ibsen, William Archer) provided him with a framework within which he was able to develop his own distinctive style as a dramatist. Equally important as a background to his plays was his engagement with the intellectual, political, religious, and social issues of the second half of the nineteenth century. It was to this period, which he names in the Preface to *Heartbreak House* "The Wicked Half Century" (18), that Shaw traced the origins of the social malaise explored in his play and the catastrophic crisis in history that was reached with the outbreak of World War I.

The last 50 years of the nineteenth century was a period of immense upheaval and conflict in every major area of social life. The evolutionary theories of Darwin, set forth in *The Origin of Species* (1859) and *The Descent of Man* (1871), not only contributed to a profound unsettling of religious faith but also provided, in the opinion of Shaw and others, a philosophical underpinning of ruthlessly exploitative systems of capitalist enterprise and cynical acceptance of the law of survival of the fittest as a governing principle of human conduct. The enormous expansion of European imperial dominions led to territorial and economic rivalry and conflict, which could be described as a form of social Darwinism on an international scale. In the meantime, the writings of Karl Marx were throwing out a challenge to the entire economic and social structure of Russia and the West, which was to bring in its wake in England various socialist movements to one of which Shaw attached himself. As Shaw was writing *Heartbreak House*, a major outcome of the revolutionary work of Marx and his followers—the overthrow of the czar and the collapse of monarchic rule in Russia—was taking place. But England was still very much in the power of capitalist bosses such as Mangan in Shaw's play; its class system was still firmly entrenched, and its empire was vast.

In the early 1880s Shaw joined several debating and discussion societies, and in September 1884 he was elected to membership of the recently founded Fabian Society, in which he soon became one of the leading executive members. The Fabians aimed to create in Britain a democratic socialist state. Their strategy was to bring about the gradual permeation of existing political groups with socialist ideas. The Fabian Society was also influential in the founding of the British Labour party in the early years of the twentieth century.

The nineteenth-century debates about evolution influenced Shaw's entire outlook on life, and the writing of *Heartbreak House* reflects that influence in more than one way. In tune with the Fabian ideal of gradual political reform was Shaw's new "religion," as he called it, of Creative Evolution. Shaw conceived of the godhead not as a stable, unchanging entity but as a constantly evolving phenomenon, immanent in the universe, which he called the Life Force. The divine is located in the mysterious forces of life that are involved in evolutionary processes, and individuals are capable of influencing the development of these processes. Paradoxically, however, these ideas are often coupled in Shaw's thinking with powerful strains of skepticism about the possible reformability of human nature and with denunciations, reminiscent of Jonathan Swift in *Gulliver's Travels*, of the whole of humankind. Like his younger contemporary, D. H. Lawrence, Shaw sometimes contemplated the replacement of the human species by a new order of beings altogether. This notion finds its way into *Heartbreak House* in one of Hector's speeches near the beginning of act 3 after a "splendid drumming in the skies" is heard: "Either out of that darkness some new creation will come to supplant us as we have supplanted the animals, or the heavens will fall in thunder and destroy us" (159).

Shaw's attachment to progressive and meliorist causes and ideas such as Fabian Socialism and Creative Evolution was sometimes combined with a baffling and seemingly anarchic propensity to dismantle his own intellectual edifices. Eric Bentley, in his study of Shaw, remarked that *Heartbreak House* could be described as "the Nightmare of a Fabian . . . a picture of failure."[4] Certainly the dark comedy and apocalyptic images of the final scene of the play seem a far cry from the reformist platforms of Fabianism, and the motif of Creative Evolution is heard here only in a most negative key. But such darker sides of the Shavian vision are not, as Bentley's comment might suggest, an entirely new development in Shaw's outlook. More than a decade before this, in the Dream in Hell sequence of his play *Man and Superman* (1901–1903), Shaw armed the dream persona of the Devil with some of the most powerfully skeptical and cynical writing about man—and his skill in the "arts of death"—in the Shavian canon. The image of the Shaw of *Heartbreak House* as an erstwhile cheery Fabian who had suddenly found his illusions shattered by the horror of World War I is an oversimplification of his earlier intellectual outlook. Nevertheless, the outbreak of World War I, as well as events in his private life, did precipitate a complex crisis in Shaw's career that left a deep imprint on the shape and temper of *Heartbreak House.*

World War I, and Shaw's participation in fierce debate about its causes, were of major importance as contextual factors in the creation of *Heartbreak House.* By the time of the war's outbreak Shaw had clearly established himself as the leading playwright of his day in England, with a very strong international reputation. He had captivated and conquered the London to which he had come in 1876 as an unknown, impoverished, and unemployed young Irishman. By the end of 1914, however, his relationship with the British public had undergone a dramatic change.

Shaw's first action on hearing of the war's outbreak was to send a cable to his German translator, Siegfried Trebitsch. Trebitsch, a gentle and mildly mannered Austrian novelist and playwright, had met Shaw in 1901, and the two had subsequently formed a close friendship, collaborating on numerous projects of translation, and German productions, of Shaw's works. The language of Shaw's message to Trebitsch anticipates the apocalyptic notes of *Heartbreak House*: "WHAT A HIDEOUS SITUATION CIVILISATION TEARING ITSELF TO PIECES . . . YOU AND I AT WAR CAN ABSURDITY GO FURTHER" (*Letters*, 3:243). Overnight, the two friends and intellectual collaborators and their wives had officially become enemy aliens. There could hardly have been a more striking instance of the helplessness of cultivated, intelligent people in the face of the huge groundswell of political and economic forces, imperial rivalries, and international power struggles that culminated in World War I.

In the last months of 1914—as war fever, jingoism, and anti-German feeling mounted, as a massive campaign of voluntary recruitment got under way, as women were exhorted on hoardings to encourage their sons to serve king and country, as the air was filling with patriotic songs such as the one that Randall plays on his flute at the end of *Heartbreak House*, as panic spread with tens of thousands of Belgian refugees pouring into the country with exaggerated tales of German atrocities and as thousands of young men were already being slaughtered at the front—Shaw sat down to write a polemical pamphlet that went completely against the grain of the national mood. His 35,000-word essay, "Common Sense about the War," was published as a special supplement to the left-wing periodical the *New Statesman* in mid-November. Predictably enough, the essay provoked hostility from all quarters: the public reaction at the time is summed up as follows by Dan H. Laurence:

> *Common Sense about the War* shook the nation to its underpinnings, generating a fury of outrage and splenetic derogation from the press. He was denounced as a traitor, an enemy "within our walls." Former friends cut him dead at committee meetings and in the streets. Booksellers and librarians removed his works from their shelves. Socialist colleagues took up the cry, with one of them . . . describing *Common Sense about the War* as "insensate malice and dirty innuendo" and its authorship as

"the meanest act of treachery ever perpetrated by an alien
enemy residing in generous and long-suffering England."
(*Letters*, 3:239–40)

The official immediate justification for Britain's declaration of
war was Germany's violation of Belgian neutrality, as its forces tram-
pled over its neighbor in the march toward the campaign with the old
enemy, France. Shaw's position was not that of a pacifist, but he saw
the violation of Belgian neutrality as a pretext for a war that was essentially a struggle for supremacy between rival European imperial powers, promoted by junker militarist classes in Britain, Prussia, and
elsewhere. His pamphlet was just as critical of British politicians and
what he saw as their devious ways of presenting the issues as it was of
Prussian militarists. There was an infuriating Irish neutrality in Shaw's
"common sense" about the war.

The drift of the world into a war of "civilisation tearing itself to
pieces" obviously had a major influence on the shaping of the moods
of anger, near-despair, and foreboding expressed in *Heartbreak House*.

The Shaw house at Ayot St. Lawrence in Hertfordshire was
close to the flight paths of the zeppelins, the cigar-shaped, hydrogen-
filled airships the Germans had begun to employ in bombing raids on
English towns and cities since December 1914. The zeppelins were
capable of a speed of only about 20 miles an hour, and the drumming of their engines must have lingered in the air for very considerable periods of time. On the night of 1 October 1916 an L31
zeppelin bound for London flew directly over Shaw's house, "with
the nicest precision . . . straight along our ridge tiles," as Shaw put it
in a letter to Sidney and Beatrice Webb a few days later (*Letters*, 3:
425). The zeppelin was successfully attacked from beneath by a fight-
er plane and descended slowly as a huge fireball to the ground near
Potters Bar, a village to the south of Ayot St. Lawrence. Shaw wit-
nessed the spectacle, and traveled by motorbike to Potters Bar to see
the wreckage.

As was first pointed out by Arthur H. Nethercot in 1966, a passage in Shaw's letter to the Webbs directly anticipates the extraordi-

nary mood of exhilaration that accompanies the violent close of *Heartbreak House* and contains the seed of the idea of Nurse Guinness's *"hideous triumph"* at the annihilation of Billy Dunn and Mangan in the gravel pit:

> What is hardly credible, but true, is that the sound of the Zepp's engines was so fine, and its voyage through the stars so enchanting, that I positively caught myself hoping next night that there would be another raid. I grieve to add that after seeing the Zepp fall like a burning newspaper, with its human contents roasting for some minutes (it was frightfully slow) I went to bed and was comfortably asleep in ten minutes. One is so pleased at having seen the show that the destruction of a dozen people or so in hideous terror and torment does not count. "I didnt half cheer, I tell you" said a damsel at the wreck. Pretty lot of animals we are. (*Letters*, 3:426)

In this extraordinarily candid passage, Shaw's response to immediate events in the war came into very close touch with some of the imaginative depths and psychological insights of *Heartbreak House*.

A few months before the zeppelin incident there occurred another episode in Shaw's wartime experiences that also has significance as part of the sociohistorical context of the play. The initial inspiration for the writing of *Heartbreak House* almost certainly came to Shaw in 1913 when the actress Lena Ashwell was telling him stories about her father, Commander Pocock, a sea captain who, after an adventurous life in various parts of the world, took to living with his family on a sailing ship that he fitted out as a home, complete with nursery, drawing room, and greenhouse. But in a letter he wrote to Virginia Woolf very late in his life, Shaw gave another account of the conception of *Heartbreak House*.

Shaw began writing *Heartbreak House* on 4 March 1916.[5] That June, Virginia and Leonard Woolf joined the Shaws and Sidney and Beatrice Webb for a weekend stay at a country house, called Wyndham Croft, in Sussex (the southern county in which *Heartbreak House* is set). Writing to Virginia Woolf in 1940, Shaw said, "There is a play of mine called Heartbreak House which I always connect with you because I conceived it in that house somewhere in Sussex where I first met you and, of course, fell in love with you. I suppose every man did" (*Letters*, 4:557).[6] Shaw had obviously forgotten that he had already begun writing *Heartbreak House* before this meeting with the Woolfs, but this does not detract from the interest of the letter as an evocation of the social world with which Shaw associated the play.

He must have felt a curious conjunction between art and life on that weekend in Sussex. He was probably writing *Heartbreak House* in the garden at Wyndham Croft in the mornings.[7] At the same time he was one of a gathering in a country house of some of the most intelligent and cultivated people in the land, powerless to do anything except talk and, as Shaw's letter suggests, flirt, while civilization was "tearing itself apart" all around them. The letter to Virginia Woolf is also of interest in its inclusion of the Bloomsbury circle in the portrait of upper middle-class English society *Heartbreak House* presents.

More specific echoes in the play of this meeting with the Woolfs have been proposed. As Stanley Weintraub suggests, the ex-colonial civil servant Leonard Woolf may have unwittingly contributed to the creation of the important offstage character in the play—the colonial governor, Hastings Utterword. Less convincing is the notion that Virginia Woolf served as a model for Ariadne Utterword; though there may be some recollection in the character of Woolf's aloof manner and attractiveness (Weintraub, 165). In terms of Ariadne's act 3 disquisition on the division of good society in England into the equestrian classes and the neurotic classes, Virginia Woolf would seem a more likely model for the latter class, rather than the former, to which Ariadne clearly sees herself as belonging.

2

The Importance of *Heartbreak House*

Heartbreak House presents a powerful and disturbing yet highly entertaining portrait of a society in decay and a world that may be on the brink of doom. It deals with the grimmest of themes yet is punctuated throughout with trenchant and sardonic wit and amusing but not merely diverting surprises and comic situations. It is about heartbreak, violence, and social disorder yet lends itself to descriptions such as that of one of its first reviewers in 1920 in New York who found it "quite the larkiest and most amusing [play] that Shaw has written in many a year."[1] (The reviewer had evidently forgotten that Shaw's previous full-length play was one of his best comedies, *Pygmalion*.) *Heartbreak House* includes in its speculative range the possible annihilation of the human race, yet its temper remains ebullient and sharply funny. It is in these conflicting energies of dark portent and often wild comedy that much of the force of the play lies.

Since its first publication in 1919 *Heartbreak House* has retained a remarkable, and indeed sinister, topicality and relevance. Major revivals have been presented in each decade since the 1920s, and a recurring feature of reviews has been comment on the way in which the play "always seems to have something new to say to the generation seeing it."[2] The play must have had an uncomfortable pertinence to audiences at the Mercury Theater in New York in 1938 as the world watched the events that were to lead up to the beginning of a new worldwide holocaust the following year. In 1943, when it was played in London during the air raids, audiences had to be advised in a program note of the procedures to be adopted if an actual air raid were to occur during the performance of the play.

Although he begins his Preface by saying that Heartbreak House is "cultured, leisured Europe before the war," in the play Shaw took care to avoid any specific reference to World War I or the date of the action. His opening stage direction simply specifies "a fine evening at the end of September." In the program for a production at the Old Vic Theatre in Bristol the date "1914" was added to Shaw's prescription about the setting. The director of a production at the Glasgow Citizens' Theatre in 1985 went further and introduced into the play a quartet of World War I British soldiers who appeared from time to time in full battle dress marching or running across the stage amongst the hosts and guests of *Heartbreak House*. But such overt orientations tend to reduce the potential resonances of the "splendid drumming in the sky" and the capacity of the work to represent "cultured, leisured" Anywhere, at any time.

To say this is not, however, to deny the play's obvious connections with early twentieth-century history or the significance of World War I as part of the matrix in which the work was conceived.

Apart from its continuing topicality, *Heartbreak House* has a number of other claims to the title "masterwork." The artistic organization of the play is complex and subtle. In less skilful hands such a diffuse, rambling, and often inconclusive series of narrative strands as those developed in *Heartbreak House* would be extremely hazardous. But in the theater, when properly performed, the play reveals a remarkably taut construction. The cruel games of flirtation, manipulation, rejection, and exposure played out in the Shotover household cumulatively create an atmosphere of high tension that is released, though not entirely dispensed with, in the play's tumultuous last scene.

From its beginnings as a playful portrait of an eccentric household in Sussex and a tale of romantic disappointment, the play develops powerful metaphorical dimensions. It unfolds as a wide-ranging and imaginative diagnosis of a disordered, directionless society, of lives wasted in foolish pursuits, of the disjunction between culture and intelligence on the one hand and the seats of power in government, capital, and empire on the other. At the same time it presents a unique perspective on the nature of heartbreak itself, and on the cultural assumptions that underlie the concept. The critic Desmond MacCarthy, who maintained that Shaw was deficient in his understanding of heartbreak,[3] does less than justice to the way in which this play explores the idea of heartbreak and invests the term with new meaning.

3

Critical Reception

The early critical reception of *Heartbreak House* was very mixed in character. When the work was first published in 1919 some reviewers cast doubt on whether it was playable in the theater.[1] An old intellectual sparring partner of Shaw's, A. B. Walkley, complained that the play contained too much recycled Shavian material but conceded that "the pamphleteer in him [Shaw] is surpassed by the artist" (Evans, 242). Memorably characterizing the play as "half-procession, half-pandemonium," leading journalist and critic John Middleton Murry predicted that it could be "intensely amusing" onstage but took Shaw to task for attempting to equate the malaise and futility of the Russian intelligentsia with that of the English (Evans, 244).

When the play came to be presented in New York and London, newspaper critics greeted it with some bewilderment and a considerable amount of hostility. This does not seem to have altogether discouraged audiences, as the play had 125 performances in New York and 63 in London. But the early reviews contained frequent complaints about length (because of a technical problem the play ran for nearly four hours at its London premiere) and verbosity. One of the most severe critics described the work as "four hours of a political

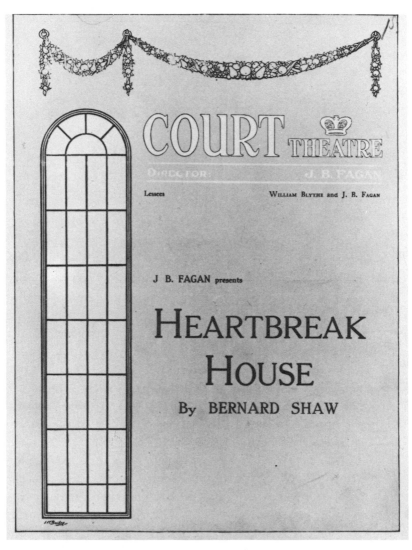

Cover of program for first U.K. production of *Heartbreak House*, Royal Court Theatre, London, 1921. *Photograph from the Victoria and Albert Collection. Used with kind permission of the Theatre Museum, London.*

tract . . . this latest of Bleak Houses" and reported that one old gentleman in the audience remained fast asleep even during the explosion of the bomb in the final scene.[2]

Yet among the early reviews there were clear signs that at least some of the critics were aware of the play's importance. Desmond MacCarthy, a penetrating early commentator on Shaw, remarked that *Heartbreak House* needed only a blue pencil and a pair of scissors to turn it into "a masterpiece."[3] This was the first of many occasions that theater critics applied the term to the work. More than 20 years later MacCarthy saw a very good production of the play and wrote, "When *Heartbreak House* is as well performed as it is at the Cambridge Theatre, it is one of the most excitingly amusing and interesting of Shaw's plays."[4] The strikingly mixed reviews of the first New York and London productions are epitomized in the notice of the play by James Agate in the 21 October 1921 London *Saturday Review*. Agate referred to the plot as "an affair of grotesque and horrid accouplements" and declared that "as an entertainment pure and simple it is dull and incoherent." By the end of the review, however, Agate reports, "I found [the play] quite definitely exhilarating and deeply moving, and it therefore ranks for me among the great testaments."

Subsequent theatrical reviews of *Heartbreak House* have been very much more evenly positive in tone than those that greeted the first New York and London productions of the play. Two years after the London premiere it was produced by the Birmingham Repertory Theatre Company, and this first revival was declared by one reviewer to be "a masterly production of a masterpiece."[5] Since the 1920s major professional productions of the play have been staged in Great Britain and the United States in each decade of the century, and there have been many important revivals in other locations worldwide. When the American critic Daniel C. Gerould saw the play in Moscow in 1967, the production had been running for six years.[6]

Highlights of the play's more recent history in the theater have included the much acclaimed Old Vic production under the direction of John Schlesinger in 1975, which featured, among other notable moments, "a superbly resonant, ominous, Aeschylean chorus effect from the widely spaced figures of Captain Shotover, Hector and

Hesione chanting in the almost dark" at the end of act 1.[7] Rex Harrison played the role of Shotover, with Diana Rigg as Hesione and Mel Martin as Ellie at the Haymarket in London in 1983, and Harrison repeated the role in a production at Circle in the Square in New York later that same year. A notable production was given at the Glasgow Citizens' Theatre in 1985, and the 1980s also saw fine productions in Melbourne and Sydney, Australia. In 1992 the play was presented at the Theatre Royal in London with a distinguished cast headed by Paul Scofield as Shotover and Vanessa Redgrave as Hesione.[8] A televised version of the play, based on the 1983–84 Circle in the Square production, was prepared for cable television's "Broadway on Showtime" series in the United States in 1985.

Heartbreak House has attracted vast academic critical and interpretative commentary. Academic criticism of Shaw contrasts quite sharply with his reception in the theater. Since the early years of the twentieth century Shaw's work has remained firmly entrenched as a major force in the theatrical repertory of Great Britain, the United States, and Canada. By contrast, at mid-century he was largely locked out of the dominant critical discourses in academia. Apart from the works on Shaw by G. K. Chesterton (who does not comment on *Heartbreak House*), fuller length critical study of the plays up until the late 1940s is of little value. In this period far more interesting material is to be found in theater reviews.

Eric Bentley's pioneering *Bernard Shaw* (1947) marks the beginning of serious post–World War II study of the playwright's work. Bentley treats *Heartbreak House* as one of a group of three works that, borrowing a term from Shaw, he calls "disquisitory plays" (Bentley, 87ff). The first work in the group was *Getting Married* (1908), which Shaw had subtitled "A Disquisitory Play," and the second was *Misalliance*, which he subtitled threateningly "A Debate in One Sitting." Bentley was right to see a family resemblance between these three works, but he fails to be sufficiently circumspect about Shaw's comic subtitles as definitions of the generic character of the plays.

Shaw's subtitles were clearly part of an ironically conducted polemical campaign against those early critics who refused to regard his works as real plays. The use of terms such as "disquisitory" and "debate" tends to obscure the skillfully developed underpinnings of action in this group of plays. The action is sometimes sensational—as when an airplane crashes into a greenhouse or Mr. Tarleton finds himself confronted with a socialist burglar in his portable Turkish bath in *Misalliance*—and sometimes more subtle, as in the continual interpersonal power struggles in both *Misalliance* and *Heartbreak House*. A great deal is going on beneath the torrents of words in all three of these plays.

Bentley's comments about the allegorical significance of the characters in *Heartbreak House* has had some currency in later discussion. Bentley adopts the suggestion of another critic that four allegorical figures in a much later Shaw play, *The Simpleton of the Unexpected Isles*, have their counterparts in *Heartbreak House*. Thus, in this account Hesione is Love, Ariadne is Empire, Randall is Pride, and Hector is Heroism. But this again is problematic, and Bentley acknowledges the inadequacy of such equations as "reductive" (Bentley, 95). Attempts to put the characters into such molds of abstraction bring to mind Mary McCarthy's brilliant aperçu about the "nightmarish fluidity" of the characterization in *Heartbreak House*.

Mary McCarthy, writing in 1938, was conscious that something radically new was created in Shavian drama in *Heartbreak House*—a new sense not only of lost characters but also of a "lost author, who could not, in conscience, make his story come out right, or, indeed, come out at all."[9] Similarly, Edmund Wilson in *The Triple Thinkers* stressed the new quality of *Heartbreak House*: "There is no diagram of social relations, no tying up of threads at the end."[10] But it must be said that this can also be applied to a number of earlier Shaw plays, many of which end on ambiguous notes.

A good deal of critical attention has been devoted to the unusual structure of the play. This was one of the concerns of F. P. W. McDowell, whose penetrating essay "Technique, Symbol, and Theme in *Heartbreak House*" was an important landmark in academic study of the work.[11] McDowell finds in the play's "simmering tensions" a "carefully modulated looseness" that he relates to the musical fantasia, invoked by Shaw in the subtitle of the play. (The fantasia analogy has been further explored by Martin Meisel and Michael W. Kaufman, among others.)[12] McDowell further comments on Shaw's skillful creation of "a stylised imaginative world, whose relation to mundane reality is only tangential." He touches also on the much-debated question of the Burglar episode and finds the introduction of the Burglar to be "a structural blemish"; still, the episode has been strongly defended by some critics since.

The idea that *Heartbreak House* is intended to be understood as a dream taking place within the subconscious mind of Ellie, after she dozes off while reading Shakespeare at the beginning of act 1, was first proposed by C. B. Purdom in 1963 and has been commented on by several critics since.[13] Margery M. Morgan subtitled her sensitive and suggestive chapter on the play in *The Shavian Playground* "Shaw's Dream Play,"[14] and her epigraph to this study of the play is drawn from Strindberg's introduction to his *A Dream Play*, the organization and experiential texture of which is intended to reflect the experience of dreaming. Certainly the action and atmosphere of *Heartbreak House* have surreal dimensions, and the motif of dreaming recurs, as, for example, in the episode in act 2 when Mangan is hypnotized by Ellie. But I agree with Peter Ure that the idea that the whole play is Ellie's dream "hardly seems to work out."[15]

A strong upsurge of interest in Shaw in the 1960s and 1970s was manifested in the publication of a large number of book-length critical studies of his work as a dramatist, including those by Charles A. Carpenter, Louis Crompton, Elsie B. Adams, Margery M. Morgan, Charles A. Berst, Maurice J. Valency, J. L. Wisenthal, Alfred Turco, R. F. Whitman, and myself.[16] Most of these studies include extensive critical discussion of *Heartbreak House*, and they display a broad consensus about the high quality of the work—a judgment exemplified in Louis Crompton's description of it as "unsurpassed in the Shavian canon for the subtlety of its art, its depth of poetic feeling, and the fascination of its symbolism" (Crompton, 168).

The play has continued to have its detractors, however, and there are those who, while respectful of the work, have serious reservations about its artistic success. Stark Young, for example, having previously decided with Edmund Wilson that *Heartbreak House* was Shaw's best play, was disappointed by the Orson Welles production at the Mercury Theater in 1938 (a generally very well-received production) and 10 years later declared the play to be "garrulous, unfelt and tiresome."[17] Others who have expressed reservations about the quality of the work include J. I. M. Stewart, Homer E. Woodbridge, and Nicholas Grene.[18]

In *Bernard Shaw:A Critical View* Nicholas Grene brought a welcome evaluative rigor to critical study of Shaw, and his discussion of *Heartbreak House* presents a challenge to those who highly value this work. He finds some real merits in the play—the conception of some of the characters, especially Hesione (who, I would agree, is one of Shaw's finest character creations), the "vitality of comic dialogue," and "the composition of individual scenes"—but generally he finds the play lacking in coherence and "only very partially successful" (Grene, 131).

Certainly it is possible to sympathize, if not necessarily agree, with some of Grene's critical reservations about *Heartbreak House*. It is understandable that in a reading (though not, I think, when it is well performed) the play might be seen as "overcrowded" (Grene, 119), but some of the assumptions underlying this criticism are problematic. In the early part of his chapter Grene announces his project as being "to see how well the post-Chekhovian mode of the play's form and technique suited Shaw, and whether we can really find in it the signs of a new tragic vision in his work" (Grene, 115). Here the problem is that the question is invented by the critic and not essentially prompted by the work. Shaw describes *Heartbreak House* as a "Fantasia," and whatever other generic mode the play might suggest it is certainly not that of any conventional form of tragedy. In the Preface Shaw refers unequivocally to the play as a "comedy" (56): *Heartbreak House* does not present itself for judgment as a work of "tragic vision."

A further problem with Grene's analysis is his complaint about what he calls Shaw's "disregard for the *liaison des scènes*" (Grene, 117). He finds in the play a lack of dramatic continuity and describes act 2 as a "relentless sequence of unrelated emotional fireworks" (Grene, 116, 117). The fireworks are not strictly unrelated, but, more importantly, I think it can be argued that the sense of fitful activity and discontinuity conveyed in the dramatic narratives is germane to its portrait of social disintegration and disorder. Fitfulness, abrupt changes of direction, and precipitous entrances and exits such as those of Captain Shotover in quest of or returning from his rum are part of the play's essential aesthetic character. *Heartbreak House* is a deliberately disconcerting play.

In his *Journey to Heartbreak: The Crucible Years of Bernard Shaw, 1914–1918* (1971) Stanley Weintraub provides a useful biographical account of Shaw's controversial and extraordinarily eventful career during World War I. In an appendix to his work Weintraub examines some of the connections between *Heartbreak House* and Shakespeare's *King Lear*. My analysis of the connections between the two plays in Chapter 4 is placed in the context of a more wide-ranging study of the intertextual relations of *Heartbreak House* and shows the complexity and parodic character of Shaw's use of Shakespeare in the play.

The textual history of *Heartbreak House*, as with many of Shaw's plays, is complicated. Shaw was a frequent and assiduous reviser of his works, and in a large number of cases we have evidence of several stages of composition, including manuscripts and typescripts, amended proof copies, and amended copies of published works. Shaw ordered the cutting of 65 lines of act 3 of *Heartbreak House* after the opening of the first London production.[19] It would be extremely difficult to represent all the revisions in a critical edition of his works, and no such edition exists. In many ways this is unfortunate because it means that many significant phases of composition (for example, the original and superior ending of *Pygmalion*) are becoming lost to view. A facsimile of the typescript of *Heartbreak House*, with numerous revisions by Shaw, has been edited by Stanley Weintraub and Anne Wright, but valuable as this edition is, it does not adequately indicate the important further revisions Shaw made at the proof stage.

Anne Wright has also made important contributions to understanding Shaw's play in two other publications—her book *Literature of Crisis, 1910–1922* and the earlier article "Shaw's Burglars: *Heartbreak House* and *Too True to Be Good*."[20] In *Literature of Crisis* she examines *Heartbreak House* in relation to E. M. Forster's *Howards End*, D. H. Lawrence's *Women in Love*, and T. S. Eliot's *The Waste Land*, arguing that in different ways these works all reflect a sense of radical and alarming change and imminent catastrophe in human history in the second and third decades of the twentieth century. In "Shaw's Burglars" she argues convincingly that the Burglar episode in *Heartbreak House* is not dramatically unmotivated and that the Burglar's entry "bodies forth a cluster of latent ideas about the relationships of the characters, generating a metaphoric language which permeates the texture of the play" (Wright 1980, 2). She points out that "after his intrusion images of stealing, selling and imprisonment steadily inform the action" (Wright 1980, 2).

In *Literature of Crisis* Wright relates her chosen texts to Frank Kermode's concept of "the modern apocalypse,"[21] seeing them as each displaying a sense of crisis, "expressed as the fracturing or dismantling of personal relations, of social institutions, of civilisations" (Wright 1984, 3). Wright attributes to these texts a more purposive, teleological design than any of them can strictly bear, and she does not, I think, sufficiently discriminate between the different character of the responses to crisis expressed by the four authors.

There are certainly some clear parallels between *Howards End* and *Heartbreak House*. Forster calls England a "ship of souls,"[22] and there is the threat of doom in his evocation of Beethoven's music as in Shaw's. Both works are concerned with money and power and the divorce between culture and power. But the perspectives on the "condition of England" in Forster's work are radically different from those of Shaw in *Heartbreak House*. Forster's novel reflects a nostalgic longing for an older, gentler England, before the arrival of the offensive motorcar and the civilization of hurry and disorder. Shaw's play reflects no such desires.

It must likewise be said that the apocalyptic notes of Eliot (as of Yeats) are in a quite different key from those of Shaw. Oddly enough, it is D. H. Lawrence's *Women in Love*, with its vision of the possible replacement of the human race by another species and its ferocious treatment of capitalist bosses, that, among the works considered by Wright, comes closest to *Heartbreak House* in spirit. Wright makes illuminating comments on *Heartbreak House*, especially in regard to its treatment of gender relations and the tendency of the female characters as a group to reduce the males to a state of "infantilism."[23] Her discussion of the way in which the play generates uncertainty about its own end (Wright 1984, 93, 106–108) is apt and penetrating.

Readers of *Heartbreak House* may sometimes be put in mind of Samuel Johnson's remark about Milton's *Paradise Lost*, that "none ever wished it longer than it is." Although *Heartbreak House* is a mere short story in comparison with Milton's epic, by contemporary standards it is a long play, and complaints about the length, especially of act 2, have recurred in critical comments. Nevertheless, *Heartbreak House* has continued to impress audiences and fascinate critical commentators for 80 years. The play shows that sure sign of distinction in a literary work—that it continues to reward critical inquiry after a very long period since its first appearance. It is standing the ultimate—and probably the only decisive—test of literary merit, that of time, very well.

A READING

4

A Chamber of Echoes

Heartbreak House is the site of a remarkably complex convergence of creative impulses and influences. The play reflects an intricate intertwining of some of Shaw's personal experiences in the pre–World War I period with his responses to literary and dramatic texts. These experiences and responses became linked, in turn, with the larger "text" of early twentieth-century history. As Europe was stumbling toward the most destructive war, up to that time, in human history, certain turbulent situations were developing in Shaw's private life that were to shape some of the central thematic concerns and images of *Heartbreak House*, especially in regard to the treatment of sexual and filial relations.

In the same period Shaw had his one meeting with August Strindberg, whose treatments of marital relations in his plays and stories find parallels in *Heartbreak House*, and saw the first London production of one of Strindberg's plays about that subject, *Creditors*. He was also extolling the virtues of Anton Chekhov, one of the Russian masters alluded to in *Heartbreak House*'s subtitle, "A Fantasia in the Russian Manner on English Themes" ("everything we write in England seems sawdust after Tchekhov" [*Letters*, 3:439]), and was helping to get the Russian's work on the English stage. And he was also apparently reimmersing himself in the texts of *Othello* and *King Lear*—plays that figure prominently in the intertextual relations of *Heartbreak House*.

This chapter does not aim at an encyclopedic account of the numerous echoes of other texts present in *Heartbreak House*. Nor does it set out to deny that the play is very much preoccupied with the kinds of "public" themes—the predicament of "cultured, leisured Europe before the war" (12), the disastrous separation of culture and power in English and European societies, the failure of the intellectual elites, and their part in the "drift to the abyss" (21)—that are so much highlighted by Shaw in his 1919 Preface. My aim here is to explore the patterns of intertextual play and creative dialogue with other texts that are discernible in *Heartbreak House*, as well as the ways in which these patterns can be seen to relate to key aspects of Shaw's biography in the early years of the twentieth century. The autobiographical and intertextual dimensions of the play are close to some of its main centers of dramatic energy and interest. Although they are intricately connected with one another, I shall treat these two dimensions of *Heartbreak House* separately.

THE BIOGRAPHICAL MATRIX

Shaw's sexually unconsummated marriage of companionship with Charlotte Payne-Townshend, entered into in 1898, was placed under severe strain by two relationships he had with other women in the early years of the next century. The most celebrated of these was his affair with the "perilously bewitching"[1] Stella Campbell—one that, for all its moments of high comedy, was also the most serious emotional entanglement of his life. Beatrice Rose Stella Campbell—Mrs. Patrick Campbell as she was professionally known—scored her first triumphs as an actress on the London stage in the 1890s, at the time Shaw was drama critic for the *Saturday Review*. Shaw was enchanted by her and, while heaping scorn on many of the plays in which she was cast, lavished praise on her Circean charms as an actress. Of her playing in the title role in Pinero's *The Notorious Mrs. Ebbsmith*, he wrote, "She creates all sorts of illusions and gives one all sorts of searching sensations. It is impossible not to feel that those haunting eyes are brooding on a momentous past, and the parted lips anticipating a thrilling imminent future, whilst some enigmatic present must no less surely be working underneath all that subtle play of limb and stealthy intensity of tone" (*Theatres*, 1:61).

The "searching sensations" were destined to remain with Shaw for a very long time, eventually blossoming into passionate love some 17 years later. The famous correspondence between the two began in 1899, the year after Shaw's marriage. Shaw's first letter to Mrs. Pat, inviting her to join the recently wed couple at a rented house in Hindhead, contained what was to become a deeply ironic second sentence: "Mrs. Shaw will be delighted to see you" (*Correspondence*, 11). As things were to turn out, Mrs. Patrick Campbell was to become about the last person Mrs. Charlotte Shaw would be delighted to see. In June 1912 Shaw read his new play, *Pygmalion*, to Stella, the future player of Eliza Doolittle, at her home in Kensington. Two days later he wrote his friend Harley Granville Barker to say he had fallen "violently and exquisitely in love" (*Letters*, 3:95). In his letters to Stella he was soon rapturously addressing her as "Beatricissima" (most blessed) and his "Stella Stellarum" (star of stars), and the star was beginning one of her replies with "Oh darling what a letter!" (*Correspondence*, 21, 22, 27).

Stella Campbell was a highly significant figure in Shaw's creative career as well as in his personal life. She was the model for several of his leading female characters, including Hesione in *Heartbreak House*, and his affair with her is reflected in a number of ways in the treatment of the relations of the sexes and the theme of heartbreak itself in the play. Stella's personality seems to have contained practically the whole gamut of male fantasies about, and stereotyped images of, the feminine, ranging from *The Vampire*, the title of a painting by Philip Burne-Jones for which Stella was recognizably the model, to The Madonna, or "Mother of Angels," as Shaw calls her in a remarkable letter written on New Year's Eve 1913 (*Correspondence*, 154–55).[2] The vampire image is recalled in *Heartbreak House* in Hector's cry about the Shotover daughters, "Vampire women, demon women" (102), and also in one of Shaw's letters to Stella, which mentions the characters in his plays for which she was the model: "Why, oh why, do you get nothing out of me, though I get everything out of you? Mrs Hesione Hushabye in *Heartbreak House*, the Serpent in *Methuselah* . . . and Orinthia [in *The Apple Cart*]: all you, to say nothing of Eliza, who was only a joke. You are the Vamp, and I the victim; yet it is I who suck your blood" (*Correspondence*, 291).

Like the dark-haired siren Hesione in *Heartbreak House*, the dark-haired siren Stella Campbell was witty and imaginative, mischievous (she planted entries in Shaw's diary of suggested meetings with herself, which were accidentally discovered by Charlotte), flirtatious, delightfully affectionate, manipulative, and at times brutally frank and cruel. She and Shaw were experts at trading insults. Even her nickname for him, "Joey" (the name of a pantomime clown), tended, no doubt beneficially, to cut the great George Bernard Shaw down to size.

Stella Campbell unlocked emotional depths and acknowledgments of need in Shaw as no other person in his life had been able to do. To the man who prided himself on his immunity to sentimentality and romance, the relationship opened up prospects of emotional permission and gratification that seem to have been to a large extent withheld from him in his childhood. "Its good for you . . . to play in the nursery of my heart," wrote the maternal siren on 31 January 1913, after being addressed on the 29th as "loveliest doveliest babiest" (*Correspondence*, 76). This was a perilous as well as blissful situation, with psychological implications of which Shaw was quite sharply aware. He provided an acute description of his predicament in love in a 13 March 1913 letter complaining about its thralls. The mingled images of ecstasy and possible destruction are an interesting foretaste of the prevailing mood at the end of *Heartbreak House*:

> To miss the resistance that has become to me what water is to a
> fish, to hear tones in a human voice that I have never heard
> before, to have it taken for granted that I am a child and want to
> be happy, to draw the sword for the duel of sex with cunning
> confidence in practised skill and a brass breastplate, and suddenly
> find myself in the arms of a mother—a young mother, and with a

child in my own arms who is yet a woman: all this plunges me
into the wildest terror as if I were suddenly in the air thousands of
feet above the rocks or the sea . . . here I am caught up again . . .
in an ecstasy which must be delirious and presently end in my
falling headlong to destruction. (*Correspondence*, 96)

The theme touched on in this passage of the mother-woman,
under whose spell grown men become children, is one on which Shaw
had played many variations before, in works such as *Candida, Captain
Brassbound's Conversion*, and *Man and Superman*, and in his correspondence with the actress Ellen Terry. In *Heartbreak House* the
theme reaches something of a climax in the portrayal of what Boss
Mangan calls the "mothering tyranny" (167) of the women in the
Shotover household. In Shaw's 1913 letter the experience of being
unmanned and reduced to childhood is one of delight mingled with
terror and part of a shared game of Peter Pan and Wendy.[3] In the fictional world of *Heartbreak House*, however, the maternal sirens of the
household are destructive and emasculating forces; as such they resemble the character of Laura, the wife in Strindberg's *The Father*, who
came into her husband's life as "his second mother"[4] and who in the
course of the play reduces him to tearful and impotent childishness
and finally brings about his complete destruction.

In March 1912 *Creditors*, another Strindberg play, about a wife
who treats her husband as her child and brings about his destruction,
was presented by the Stage Society in London. Shortly thereafter Shaw
was writing a Preface to a new edition of his *The Quintessence of
Ibsenism*, in which he described *Creditors* as "the terrible play with
which Strindberg wreaked the revenge of the male for *A Doll's House*
[in which] it is the man who is the victim of domesticity, and the
woman who is the tyrant and soul destroyer."[5] The description by
Strindberg ("Ibsen's twin giant," as Shaw describes him in the same
Preface) of his creation of the charming tyrant mother-wife, Tekla, in
Creditors, again brings out the kinship between Shaw's portrayal of
female characters in *Heartbreak House*, especially Hesione, and that of
Strindberg in his powerful and disturbingly probing plays about marriage. "You will find the vampire wife," Strindberg wrote about Tekla

in a letter of 26 June 1892, "charming, conceited, parasitical . . . loving (two men at once!), tender, falsely maternal, in a phrase, woman as I see her!"[6]

In the summer of 1913 the Shaw-Campbell relationship moved to a point of crisis. Shaw was tormented with feelings of guilt about Charlotte, who he knew would be "heartbroken" about discoveries of the clandestine correspondence and yet who he felt was keeping him in "custody" (*Correspondence*, 79, 72). He felt "torn to bits" with "a sort of angina pectoris" but trapped in the marriage with Charlotte: "I must, it seems, murder myself or else murder her" (*Correspondence*, 117).

Since they began meeting in 1912, there had always been a strong undertow of erotic tension in Shaw's relationship with Stella, as he reveals in a comic reproach to her, months later, "Oh, her bosom! I remember now—the jade!—when she first took my hand she shook it so that it touched her bosom, an infamous, abandoned trick: it thrilled through me, through all my brass for hours" (*Correspondence*, 58). The letters and poems Shaw wrote to her reveal clearly that there was a good deal of physical dalliance in their meetings. On 8 August 1913, having seen Charlotte off to France on a holiday, he followed Stella down to the seaside in Kent, where she was staying at the Guildford Hotel, Sandwich. From his letters in the ensuing few days it is clear that they had arranged to meet to go bathing in the morning of the 11th, and that this was to be the prelude to a consummation of their affair. When he arrived at the hotel, he found that the object of his quest had fled.

It is reasonable to surmise that Shaw's feelings at the time might have been summed up by Hector's remark to Randall in *Heartbreak House* about the flirtatious behavior of Ariadne Utterword: "She makes you her servant; and when pay-day comes round, she bilks you" (156). Shaw was a jilted lover, and his letters of the next few days reveal degrees of hurt and ferocity ("I want to hurt you because you hurt me. Infamous, vile, heartless, frivolous, wicked woman! Liar! lying lips, lying eyes, lying hands, promise breaker, cheat") and self-disgust and self-pity ("Fool! Dupe! Dotard! Crybaby! . . . the wound will not heal") (*Correspondence*, 141, 143), which are without parallel in the Shaw correspondence, even though the hyperbolic expression might suggest some measure of creative delight in his *saeva indignatio*.

The "wound" of course did heal, and the relationship went on its stormy way through the rehearsals of *Pygmalion*, in the course of which Stella committed the ultimate insult of running away and marrying another George altogether—the dashing playboy with a handlebar moustache like Hector Hushabye's, George Cornwallis-West. The correspondence between Shaw and Stella continued intermittently until the year before her death in 1940. In 1937, when Shaw returned Stella's letters so that she would have them for investment purposes, he told her that he had packed them all "with infinite labour and a little heartbreak" (*Correspondence*, 313).

Shaw's perception of Stella Campbell as simultaneously "Mother of Angels" and a vampire-siren closely aligns him in this instance with the ambiguous nineteenth-century constructions of the feminine that are analyzed in Nina Auerbach's study, *Woman and the Demon: The Life of a Victorian Myth*.[7] Auerbach argues that, alongside the dominant Victorian mythography of woman as the center of domestic purity, loving subordinate of the male, and the "Angel in the House" of Coventry Patmore's popular sequence of poems in celebration of married love, there was a parallel set of myths about her regal powers and connections with the demonic. The woman of the Victorian imagination in this latter set of myths was all-powerful queen ("She-Who-Must-Be-Obeyed"),[8] serpent, vampire, destructive mermaid, and demon. Auerbach's notion that in Victorian popular and high culture "the angel can modulate almost imperceptibly into a demon" (Auerbach, 107) seems to find a clear echo in Shaw's treatment of the female characters in *Heartbreak House*.

It should be recalled here that Shaw's public stance on the feminist movement of his time—a movement that reached a point of climax in the years of suffragette activities leading up to the outbreak of World War I—was one of strong support. He entered into this debate with several powerful public statements in favor of the suffragettes and satirical attacks on their opponents.[9] The corpus of his dramatic works abounds with examples of emancipated female characters. Vivie Warren in *Mrs. Warren's Profession*, Major Barbara, Lina

Szczepanowska in *Misalliance*, Margaret Knox in *Fanny's First Play*, and Saint Joan are among the numerous Shavian female characters depicted as having made a radical break from conventional stereotypes of woman's role. But Shaw's attitude toward women was extremely complex, and in some ways *Heartbreak House* recalls the nineteenth century's ambiguous mythography of the female.

At one point near the end of act 1 Hesione presents her sex as precisely the type of the "angel in the house" in a speech: "What do men want? They have their food, their firesides, their clothes mended, and our love at the end of the day. Why are they not satisfied?" (104–105). But the solicitous mother-wife who delivers this speech is also, of course, one of the central figures in the play's construction of a female demonology. It can be argued that Ellie Dunn's progress through the play is a process of emancipation; but her portrayal is also deeply ambiguous. In letters written within a month of one another in 1921, apropos the first London production, Shaw was insisting that Ellie should appear as "perfectly virginal" and a nunlike "Bride of Christ" in her spiritual marriage with Captain Shotover but also that she is "technically the heavy lead in the play" and not its ingenue (*Letters*, 3:734, 741). Her ruthless treatment of Mangan is scarcely reminiscent of the behavior of a nunlike "Bride of Christ."

The affair with Stella Campbell probably brought Shaw as close to the experience of heartbreak as he ever came, and the relationship can be seen to have cast its spell over the composition of *Heartbreak House* in a number of ways. Shaw's experience is refracted in the presentation of several of his male characters. Critics have often located a Shavian "voice" in the character of Captain Shotover; I wish to argue instead that certain patterns of psychological experience can be seen to be distributively reflected in a number of different characters in ways that conceal their autobiographical origins, even under such unlikely disguises as the portrayals of Randall, Mangan, and Hector. By creating these comically incongruous masks of himself, Shaw was able to deal publicly, and even exuberantly, with deeply personal and painful experience.

The main paradigm of female-male relations in *Heartbreak House* is a pattern of female domination, involving mutual flirtation and sexual negotiation between male and female figures followed by exposure, humiliation and rejection of the male, and his reduction to abject states of frustration and childishness.[10] The principal victims of this pattern of behavior in the sexual politics of the play are Randall and Mangan (the two arch-victims) and Hector. But Captain Shotover is also involved in the web of female seduction and control. When Ellie takes the Captain for a walk in the garden toward the end of act 2, Hector remarks to Randall, "She has the Ancient Mariner on a string like a Pekinese dog" (149). (Stella Campbell's famous lapdogs make an early appearance in her correspondence with Shaw.) Even the Burglar in the play is discovered to have been the despised and dismissed husband of Nurse Guinness. Only the "other" Dunn, the comparatively inconsequential Mazzini, escapes more or less unscathed, though even he is reduced to tears by Hesione at one point.

Ariadne's attitude toward Randall is mainly contemptuous, but she has clearly entertained his advances over a period of many years. In act 2 she launches, in his presence, a ruthless attack on his character, describing him as "the most uninteresting man on earth" and reporting to Hector his nickname in society of "Randall the Rotter." She treats him, as though she were his mother, as a naughty "child of three," and when he breaks down and weeps under her scorn, she triumphantly labels him a "cry-baby" (154).

Hector has more defenses than Randall, but he, too, is magnetically drawn toward Ariadne. After their meeting in act 1 he accepts her invitation to a kiss, but when this becomes too passionate she suddenly pushes him away. Left alone onstage after this episode Hector (echoing Shaw's letter to Stella) curses his folly with the words, "Fool! Goat!" (98). In the context of the play's frequent references to Shakespeare's *Othello*, "goat" probably carries the sexual connotations of Othello's cry about Desdemona's supposed betrayal of him, "Goats and monkeys!" (4.1.274).

Hector has been betrayed into vulnerability and folly not only by the dangerous attractiveness of Ariadne but also by his own involuntary susceptibility: "I do not like being attracted" (97), he says to Ariadne shortly before their kiss. It is Hector who most clearly articulates the idea of the demonic character of the daughters of "that super-

Mr. Leon Quartermaine · Miss Edith Evans.
"Heartbreak House" (Queen's) 11 May 1932 : Punch

Haselden drawing from *Punch* magazine of Leon Quartermaine and Edith
Evans as Hector Hushabye and Lady Ariadne Utterword, *Heartbreak House*,
Queen's Theatre, London, 1932. *Photograph from the collections of the
Theatre Museum, London. Used with kind permission of the Punch Library
and by courtesty of the Board of Trustees of the Victoria and Albert Museum.*

natural old man," Shotover: he calls them his "demon daughters" with strange power to make men love and make them cry (96, 156). In his marriage he has clearly been reduced to lapdog status, "tied to Hesione's apron string" (103). In Captain Shotover's graphic description, Hector is "married right up to the hilt . . . at home all day, like a damned soul in hell" (142).

In one of his letters to Stella Campbell, Shaw conjures up a comically grotesque image of himself in the role of howling, spurned and betrayed suitor: "Have you ever dodged elusively round a room with a weeping, howling, red faced, swollen, aged, distorted-featured man pursuing you with a letter in his hand, pressing on you the documentary evidence in your own writing that you once loved him or pretended to?" (*Correspondence*, 107). It is possible to see in this passage an imaginative prefiguring of the sobbing, humiliated, protesting, exposed, and unprepossessing character of Mangan in *Heartbreak House*. As in the case of Randall, the play brings Mangan to a state of complete abjection. He is flirted with, ruthlessly exposed, and casually rejected. "I like him best when he is howling," Ellie remarks of him in act 3, and the *"low snivelling"* that besets him after her naming of the house as "Heartbreak House" seems to remain with him until his final disappearance from the play—*"tearfully, as he disappears"*—is the last stage direction accorded him (171, 174). Mangan is just as surely destroyed by the "mothering tyranny" of the women of Heartbreak House as by the final explosion in the gravel pit.

A further legacy of the Shaw-Campbell affair in the play can be seen in the way the theme of heartbreak itself is treated. For characters such as Randall and Mangan the experience perhaps accords with Desmond MacCarthy's idea of heartbreak as "a maiming misery" (MacCarthy, 144). For Ellie Dunn, however, it is an experience that brings new strength and tranquillity: "It is the end of happiness and the beginning of peace" (140). The unusual perspective on heartbreak in the play—the Irish logic of the idea that heartbreak is good for you—can be partly accounted for, I suggest, in biographical terms. The composition of the play can be seen as, in part, a way of exorcising the painful feelings of humiliation and rejection that Shaw had recently experienced. Life is better beyond heartbreak. Shaw's identification of

Heartbreak House with "cultured, leisured Europe before the war" in the Preface is not contradicted by the play, even though there are no specific references in the latter to this setting and time. But, as the foregoing analysis indicates, the play seems to have almost as much to do with cultured, "perilously bewitching" Stella Campbell before the war, and her stormy relationship with Bernard Shaw, as with the predicament of Europe on the brink of disaster.

In 1905, seven years before the flourishing of Shaw's affair with Stella, an intelligent, attractive, and impetuous young woman, Erica May Cotterill, became infatuated with Shaw, and, signing herself seductively as "Miss Charmer," opened up a correspondence with him by sending some of her writings for comment. Shaw was obviously flattered by the advances and adulation of this gifted and interesting young woman, and he clearly encouraged an involvement with himself that eventually became seriously threatening.[11] The charms of "Emerica" (the nickname Shaw began to use in his letters to her) were not lost on the 50-year-old playwright. But by 1909 at least, "Miss Charmer" had turned into "a quite disgustingly ill behaved young devil, grossly abusing the privilege of my acquaintance" (*Letters*, 2:847).

Erica had taken to making frequent visits to the Shaw house in London and (by motorbike) to Ayot St. Lawrence, at all hours of the day and night, and behaving, with more than friendly caresses, as though she, and not Charlotte, were the true wife of Bernard Shaw. The boldness of Erica's physical advances toward Shaw can be deduced from one of his numerous, but apparently ineffectual, lectures to her on the matter:

> In brief, if you enter my wife's house, you enter it on the understanding that you dont make love to her husband. If I introduce you to Mrs [Granville] Barker, I shall do so on the understanding that you dont make love to *her* husband. You may admire & dream & worship & adore until you are black in the face; but you are not to sit and hold their hands, nor kiss them, nor cuddle them, nor nestle in their manly bosoms—oh, so sweetly, so innocently, so heavenlikely [*sic*]—because if you do the Life Force will suddenly leap out and gobble you up. (*Letters*, 2:774–75)[12]

She had begun to behave toward Shaw in ways, he said, that he "would not stand . . . from Cleopatra herself" (*Letters*, 2:847). It was as though a vibrant young Hilda Wangel had stepped out of the pages of Ibsen's *The Master Builder* and arrived at Ayot St. Lawrence and Adelphi Terrace, demanding a great deal of attention from the master builder of English plays and master exponent of Fabian Socialist theories.[13]

The bold advances of this young woman in her early twenties toward the "elderly gentleman" (as Shaw, far from his dotage at this time, was describing himself to Erica [*Letters*, 2:732]) can hardly fail to have produced some powerful fantasies in Shaw's mind, and, as Margot Peters has noted,[14] the relationship seems clearly to have been reflected in the portrayal of the Ellie-Shotover relationship in *Heartbreak House*. The idea of a marriage between an elderly man and an attractive and imaginative young woman had been firmly lodged in Shaw's mind in a very personal way in the prewar years. When a proposal of such a marriage was put to him by Erica, with a declaration of love, in November 1907, Shaw replied with a long, platonic letter of refusal that may be seen to adumbrate the idea of the spiritual marriage of Ellie and Shotover: "As for me, I have taken declarations of love all in the day's work, as it were. They are not all illusion: there is really a divine spark in me to which the divine spark in the woman yearns: the ultimate goal of the impulse is holy" (*Letters*, 2:732). The odd moment in act 3 when Ellie precipitously announces that she has given herself to Shotover as her "spiritual husband and second father" (168), though it has its own logic in Ellie's development in the play, is partly explicable as a sanitized fictional echo of the Shaw–Cotterill relationship.

The correspondence shows that Shaw was clearly a "second father" to Erica Cotterill. She had what Shaw described much later as "a terrible hate fixation" (*Letters*, 4:638) against her own father, an undistinguished socialist headmaster and author of *Human Justice for Those at the Bottom* (1907), with whom she was locked in a state of fierce rebellion. Several of Shaw's letters take the form of counseling about her oppressive family situation and her need to break out of it. Parent-child relationships had always been a strong interest of Shaw's. At this period of his career, this interest spilled over into the enormously long Preface to *Misalliance*, "Parents and Children" (1910); into *Misalliance* itself, where the father, Tarleton, speaks of "the impassable, eternal gulf" (4:241) between parents and children and despairingly advises himself to read *King Lear*; into *Fanny's First Play* (1911), where a daughter, Margaret Knox, says of her emancipation from her family, "Ive been set free from this silly little hole of a house and all its pretences. I know now that I am stronger than you and papa" (3:396); and, finally, into *Heartbreak House*, where it becomes entangled, in more complicated ways than in *Misalliance*, with Shakespeare's treatment of the theme in *King Lear*.

THE LITERARY MATRIX

Of all writers Shaw presents himself as one of the least perturbed by the anxiety of influence. He cheerfully acknowledged his extensive pillagings from other authors—"all is fish that comes to my net"[15]—and sometimes obligingly conducts his own *Quellenforschung* in prefaces and letters. But the interaction of Shaw's plays with other texts is generally more complicated than some of his statements, suggesting primitive and unmediated piracy ("I was finding that the surest way to produce an effect of daring innovation and originality was . . . to stick closely to the methods of Molière; and to lift characters bodily out of the pages of Dickens" [258]), would lead us to think. To invoke the Bakhtinian model of the generation of meaning, his plays can be said to create a dialogic, and very frequently oppositional, relationship with other texts with which they connect.[16]

Heartbreak House is one of the most allusive of Shaw's works, and exploration of its intertextual relations involves traversing several genres. The play echoes, often in far from simple ways, a large number of other texts, from Homer to Chekhov. Allusion occurs in both explicit and implicit ways. For example, Shakespeare's *Othello* is directly referred to, or alluded to, on several occasions, but *King Lear* is an implied textual presence in the background, evoked by the image of the raging old man and his two "demon daughters" (156) and in various other indirect ways. Ironies are created by clashes between the present text and the texts echoed within it. The ending of the play, for example, might call to mind the tumultuous close of Wagner's *The Twilight of the Gods*, or the fall and burning of Troy in the classical legend. But such heroic images come into comic tension with the comparatively anticlimactic conclusion of the play, and Randall's amateurish tootling on the flute.

Characteristically, the texts of Shaw's plays bear an ironic and parodic relation to the texts and literary motifs they echo. Rather than simply borrowing from other texts, Shaw typically creates a counterdiscourse. In *Heartbreak House* this principle can be illustrated, first, by examination of the play's relation to a tradition in English nondramatic literature in which "houses" are employed metaphorically for celebration of, or critical exploration and satire of, existing social orders and mores. Shaw's first play, *Widowers' Houses*, was related to this tradition. The topos of the "house-as-ship" can be described as a subset of the larger category of these literary houses of fame, or ill-fame, and the relationship of *Heartbreak House* to the English nineteenth-century fictional tradition of shiplike houses, and to the similarly named *Bleak House* of Dickens, supplies a model of the contrapuntal, asymmetrical way in which the play echoes the texts with which it interacts.

As an avid reader of Dickens in his boyhood, Shaw would very early have come across the converted barge, situated on dry land on the foreshore, in which Mr. Peggotty and his family live at Yarmouth in *David Copperfield*. The "sort of ark" in which the good-natured Peggottys live is "beautifully clean inside, and as tidy as possible,"[17] and the Peggottys themselves are the soul of hospitality, as they attend to the needs of their young guest and conduct him to his enchanting bedroom in the stern of the vessel. In *Dombey and Son* Florence Dombey leaves the sterile dwelling of her father, and finds happiness in the shiplike house-cum-shop of the nautical instrument maker, Solomon Gills. Everything is so compactly stowed and organized in this place, where Solomon Gills lives "in skipperlike state," that "the shop itself . . . seemed almost to become a snug, sea-going, ship-shape concern, wanting only good sea-room . . . to work its way securely to any desert island in the world."[18] It is here that Florence is found a home by the hospitable friend of Gills, Captain Cuttle, in a garret "transformed into a species of land-cabin" (*DS*, 789).

Similar in character to these Dickensian shiplike houses and havens is the orderly and small but well-fitted-out house belonging to the retired Captain Harville in Jane Austen's *Persuasion*, which becomes the sanctuary for Louisa's convalescence after her fall at the Cobb in Lyme Regis. This house, with its "ingenious contrivances and nice arrangements" for which Captain Harville is responsible, looks out to sea from near the foot of an old pier. In an analysis of this house in his study of *Persuasion*, Tony Tanner remarks on the special quality of hospitality, in the best tradition of the navy, which characterizes the ordering of affairs in the Harville house.[19]

The Shotover house in Shaw's play is a travesty of these shiplike houses of order and hospitality in nineteenth-century fiction. The play gives a number of sardonic twists to the fictional tradition to which it belongs. In the opening scene an already observed but ignored guest sits reading Shakespeare in a setting that includes a carpenter's bench in the living quarters of the house, and a floor *"littered with shavings, overflowing from a waste-paper basket"* (59). The guest's luggage has been left sitting on the front steps of the house "for everybody to fall over" (62). The considerate, kindly welcome accorded David Copperfield, Florence Dombey, and Louisa Musgrove in the houses in Yarmouth, London, and Lyme Regis is here replaced by careless neglect.

The first of the play's many comments on the house and its Fawlty Towers–like management comes from an angry Captain Shotover, whose understanding of the "commonest decencies of social intercourse" (62) does not necessarily make him an exemplary practitioner: "This is a pretty sort of house, by heaven! A young and attractive lady is invited here. Her luggage is left on the steps for hours; and she herself is deposited in the poop and abandoned, tired and starving. This is our hospitality. These are our manners. No room ready. No hot water. No welcoming hostess. Our visitor is to sleep in the toolshed, and to wash in the duckpond" (62). Shortly thereafter Lady Utterword, who has had an equally unsatisfactory reception, extends the opening images of domestic chaos to deeper levels of criticism. Beneath the failings of ordinary household management she finds on her return to "this house, this house!" after a 23-year absence "the same disorder in ideas, in talk, in feeling" (65–66). The last term in this trilogy of disorders suggests a peculiarly deep-seated disorientation in the household, as though its inhabitants have lost track of basic natural codes of behavior.

In the larger tradition of fictional houses, *Heartbreak House* bears some resemblance to the satirical novels of Thomas Love Peacock, such as *Nightmare Abbey, Crotchet Castle*, and *Headlong Hall*. Set in substantial country houses, owned by enthusiastic patrons of general intellectual inquiry, Peacock's novels bring together groups of amiable eccentrics who, with much drinking of bumpers of wine, engage in vehement debate, collectively creating in each work, as one commentator aptly put it, "a madhouse . . . where there is a bee in every bonnet, but every bonnet has style."[20] Passages in *Heartbreak House*, such as Ariadne's dogmatic discourse about the advantages of houses with horse stables over those without, have a distinctly Peacockian flavor. More strongly influential on *Heartbreak House*, however, was a novel Shaw had known and admired since his teenage years, and to which he made frequent reference in his nondramatic writings—Charles Dickens's *Bleak House*.

The dwelling known as "Bleak House" in the novel belies its name: it is in fact the most cheerful dwelling of the many portrayed in the work. But the name of the house becomes a metaphor for the condition of the whole of England, as Dickens saw it, in the mid-nineteenth century, as a land of human degradation, of grinding poverty existing side by side with conditions of great wealth, and as a society in the grip of deeply corrupt and incompetent legal and political systems of management, which are the cause of widespread misery and heartbreak. Leadership in the land has failed under the direction of aristocratic personages with ludicrous names such as Coodle, Boodle, and Noodle, and the principal aristocrat in the work, the wooden Lord Dedlock, is nicknamed "Sir Arrogant Numskull," a title which probably remained in Shaw's mind when he has Shotover refer to Sir Hastings Utterword as a "numskull" (72).[21]

Maritime imagery about the state of England recurs in *Bleak House*, as in Lord Boodle's description of the country as "shipwrecked, lost and gone to pieces" (*BH*, 211). In a late passage in the novel,

England is seen as a ship, drifting without a pilot. In the same passage Dickens likens the people of England to the careless souls in the days of Noah before the apocalyptic moment of divine intervention and destruction with the flood: "England has been some weeks in the dismal state of having no pilot . . . to weather the storm; and the marvellous part is that England has not appeared to care very much about it, but has gone on eating and drinking and marrying and giving in marriage, as the old world did in the days before the flood" (*BH*, 619).[22]

The dialogue occurring just before the explosion in act 3 of *Heartbreak House* contains several ideas and images that recall such passages as those referred to here in Dickens's novel. England is again a ship, as in Hector's questioning speech, "And this ship we are all in? This soul's prison we call England?" (177). The Captain has just been talking about the dangers of a "drifting skipper" and is about to bark out his command about the proper business of an Englishman: "Navigation. Learn it and live; or leave it and be damned" (176, 177). Mazzini Dunn encapsulates the tendency of the inhabitants of Heartbreak House to avoid facing reality when he says, a second before the first explosion is heard, "I assure you nothing will happen" (177).

But for all its clear echoes of *Bleak House*, the temper of *Heartbreak House* is, finally, very different. Despite the ruin and death of Richard Carstone and the melodramatic demise of Lady Dedlock, Dickens's novel ends on a strongly upbeat note, with the happy marriage of Esther Summerson and the continued companionship of the benevolent Jarndyce: it is almost as though "there is hope for the old ship yet," to quote an ironical comment from the author-narrator in chapter 40 (*BH*, 619). But no such redemptions through love, benignity, and good fellowship are suggested by the ending of *Heartbreak House*. The pattern of Dickensian echoes is broken by the powerful counter-thrust of the completely unsentimental final movement of Shaw's "fantasia."

In his nondramatic writings Shaw—the inventor of the term "bardolatry"[23]—clearly enjoyed the sport of pulling literary giants such as Homer and Shakespeare from the pedestals on which literary history has placed them. He professed to despise Homer and reveled in denunciation of Shakespeare for having no "constructive ideas."[24]

But allusions to both Homer (or at least Homeric legend) and Shakespeare permeate *Heartbreak House* in crucially important ways. Three of the characters in *Heartbreak House*—Hesione, Hector, and Ariadne—have names that allude to classical legend. In the early typescript draft of the play Hesione bore the name Hecuba, who, in the legend of Troy, is the mother of Hector. Shaw apparently wanted to play down this overt reminder of "mothering tyranny" in the Shotover household. But the new name, of Hesione, continues the allusion to Troy in a different key. In the Trojan legend, Hesione, the sister of Priam, king of Troy, was involved in the sequence of events that led to the war and the eventual sacking and burning of Troy by the Greeks. In an earlier conflict between Greeks and Trojans, Hesione had been given by Hercules to the Greek warrior Telamon as a reward for his services in battle. The subsequent refusal by the Greeks to return her to Troy was one of the major seeds of discontent between the two races. Instead of further underlining her role as a "mother" in her relation to Hector, the new name carries an association with the beautiful females who were an essential part of the causal chain leading up to the catastrophic war and the destruction of a civilization.

Ariadne's namesake in classical mythology was associated with Aphrodite—an association perhaps recalled in Lady Utterword's amorous propensities and the fascination she holds for members of the opposite sex. But the classical Ariadne is best remembered for her brief marriage to the great hero and wandering ruler Theseus, and commentators on *Heartbreak House* are no doubt correct in discerning an echo of Theseus in the accounts of Lady Utterword's absent husband, Hastings, who has been "governor of all the crown colonies in succession" (66). Theseus is a hard-hearted and ruthless hero, and Hastings is referred to as similarly ruthless and, near the end of the play, incapable of experiencing heartbreak.

In Homer's relation of the story of Troy, Hector is the greatest of the Trojan warriors—a figure of heroic valor and military prowess whose defeat by Achilles occurs in the climactic battle of the *Iliad*. In some ways Shaw's Hector echoes this heroic figure.[25] According to Hesione's account in act 1, Hector is given to making rash demonstrations of his physical courage and has "a whole drawerful of Albert

Medals for saving people's lives" (85). But, as with so many of the allusions in the play, comic irony is present in this recollection of the great classical hero.

Shaw's Hector may have heroic qualities, but the play presents him as a mere household pet under the control of Hesione and as a largely impotent observer of the folly of both his surrounding society and his own weaknesses. His actions at the end of the play, when he rushes round the house courting further danger by turning on all the lights, may call to mind the quixotic behavior of Homer's Hector when he offers to engage in single combat with Achilles and the subsequent conflagration when, after Hector's defeat, Troy is sacked. But in *Heartbreak House* the great apocalyptic moment toward which the play tends—and which some of the characters, including Hector, positively long for—arrives in only a quite limited and rather anticlimactic way. The bomb has fallen and Mangan and the Burglar are dead, but the walls of Heartbreak House are still intact.

Shaw's dramatic and nondramatic writings show an abiding interest in, and sharp critical responses to, the works of Shakespeare. He was an eccentric but alert and engaged reader of Shakespeare, and throughout his life the Bard remained a major presence in Shaw's imagination. Works such as *The Doctor's Dilemma* and *The Dark Lady of the Sonnets* make splendid comic play with Shakespearean texts. Yet, as the tide of reverence in which Shakespeare and his works were held rose to a peak in the late nineteenth and early twentieth centuries, Shaw took great delight in shaking the pedestal on which contemporary John Bulls were placing their major cultural icon.

In his final jousting with Shakespeare, which took the form of a puppet play called *Shakes versus Shav* (1949), Shaw introduced, in explicit reference to *Heartbreak House*, a tableau based on a Millais painting of a young woman of virginal beauty sitting at the feet of an ancient sea captain, about which Shav declares, "Behold, my Lear" (475).

In *Heartbreak House* Shakespeare is alluded to even before any dialogue begins in act 1. The opening stage direction tells us that the young lady, Ellie, while impatiently waiting for some attention in the Shotover household and before she falls asleep, is passing the time by reading a copy of the Temple Shakespeare. A complex pattern of

Elizabeth Risdon as Ellie Dunn in the world premiere of *Heartbreak House*, Garrick Theater, New York, 1920. *Photograph by Ira D. Schwarz. Used by permission of the British Library.*

Shakespearean echoes is developed in the play, in which *Othello* is gradually displaced by *King Lear* as the dominant point of reference. As we learn in her first dialogue with Hesione, Ellie's perception of her romantic encounters with Hector is largely shaped by the account, in act 1, scene 3, of *Othello*, of the wooing of Desdemona by Othello with his bewitching stories of dangerous exploits and strange adventures. Ellie has been similarly enchanted by Hector's tales of his derring-do. Through Hesione, Shaw deliberately deploys the allusions to *Othello* in this scene to cast doubt on Hector's stories ("Ellie darling: have you noticed that some of those stories that Othello told Desdemona couldnt have happened?" [79]) and more generally to destabilize the margins between fiction and reality in Heartbreak House. In the course of the dialogue, Ellie displays a naive faith in both Othello and Shakespeare as truth-tellers: "Othello was not telling lies . . . Shakespear would have said if he was" (79). Hesione's dominance over the as yet ingenuous Ellie in this scene is partly defined by her obviously more intelligent, skeptical approach to the reading of Shakespeare.

The echoes of *King Lear* in *Heartbreak House* take the form of a kaleidoscopic series of refracted images, motifs, and character portraits from Shakespeare's play. It is not to the point to argue that *Heartbreak House* is some kind of botched attempt on Shaw's part at writing a Shakespearean tragedy. Kent's poignant utterance in the last moments of *King Lear*, "break heart, I prithee break" (5.3.311), may have found its echo in Shotover's command, "let the heart break in silence" (171). But Shaw's treatment of the theme of heartbreak is essentially comic in character, and the mood and temper of *Heartbreak House* is obviously quite remote from the spirit of *King Lear*. The relationship between these Shavian and Shakespearean texts is more often parodic than imitative.

The relationship between children and parents is one of several thematic loci that call for analysis in discussing the *King Lear* connections with Shaw's play. *King Lear* presents a series of radical disruptions of cultural norms in the matter of child-parent relations. Lear foolishly casts off his "joy," Cordelia, and is in turn cruelly humiliated and rejected by the "tigers, not daughters" that Goneril and Regan turn out to be. Edmund shows from the outset a contemptuous and predatory attitude toward his father, Gloucester, and sides with those who put out his eyes. The tragic pattern of *King Lear* depends on deep-rooted cultural assumptions about the "natural" relations of love and reverence that should exist between parents and children.

There is, of course, a quite straightforward reflection of *King Lear* in the images of the octogenarian, raging ("is there no thunder in heaven?" [104]) Captain Shotover and his two demonic daughters, Hesione and Ariadne. But the interaction of Shaw's text with that of *King Lear*, with respect to the treatment of the parent-child relationship, is more complicated. Early in act 1 a disconcertingly comic questioning of conventional assumptions about parent-child relations is introduced with Captain Shotover's precise assertion that "the natural term of the affection of the human animal for its offspring is six years" (64).

In one of his speeches in act 3 Shotover speaks of his deep hurt, long ago in the past, at Ariadne's running away from home when she was 19: "You left because you did not want us. Was there no heartbreak in that for your father?" (172). But the Shotover of the play's present, so far from showing a Lear-like craving for love and affection from his daughters, wishes himself rid of one and is savagely critical of the other. His railing is not about his mistreatment by his daughters but about what he sees as their wasted, foolish, and destructive lives. Like Lear, he sees his two daughters as demonic, and there are echoes of Lear's misogyny in Shotover's characterization ("they bring forth demons to delude us, disguised as pretty daughters," says Shotover in act 1 [102]). But Shotover's rage is much less focused on his own misfortune than is that of King Lear.

Hesione and Ariadne are also significantly different from their Shakespearean counterparts, the two fiendish daughters of Lear. Goneril and Regan are presented by Shakespeare as fairy tale–like figures of evil, as monsters of deceit, disloyalty, lust, and cruelty. The ruthless and cruel qualities of Hesione and Ariadne are very well in evidence in Shaw's play. Unlike Goneril and Regan, however, the two characters are of course entirely without criminal leanings, and they are also endowed with attractive, amusing and socially adroit qualities that clearly distinguish them from the Shakespearean figures.

Compared with Hesione and Ariadne, Shakespeare's Goneril and Regan are creatures of melodrama. Hesione and Ariadne are also quite different in their attitude toward the father figure. Like Lear, Shotover suffers the "casual impudence" (66) of a servant, but there is no real threat to his place in the household. Ariadne seeks Shotover's recognition and affection and is deeply hurt by his harsh response and *his* poor hospitality: in this case the tables of *King Lear* are turned. For her part, Hesione affectionately recognizes Shotover's patriarchal authority by addressing him as "Daddiest" (102).

The distribution of Shakespearean echoes in the characterization of *Heartbreak House* resembles in its complexity the way in which the prewar events in Shaw's personal life are reflected in the play. Ellie Dunn, for example, can be seen to undergo several Shakespearean metamorphoses during the play. At the beginning, as we have seen, she is closely identified with the romantically spellbound Desdemona in act 1, scene 3, of *Othello*. Following her disillusionment about "Marcus Darnley," however, a new, harder, rationalistic, and more cynical persona emerges: she becomes "as hard as nails" (122) and begins to seem more like the Goneril and Regan of *King Lear* than the Desdemona of *Othello*. In her act 2 discussion of marriage with Mangan, she is completely unromantic ("It's no use pretending we are Romeo and Juliet" [107]). When she and Hesione callously discuss Mangan as he sits, hypnotized and, as it were, blinded by Ellie, on a chair, a disturbing echo is created of the scene in *King Lear* when Goneril and Regan attend and assist in the putting out of Gloucester's eyes while he sits bound to a chair. In the last act of *Heartbreak House*, after Ellie has announced her spiritual marriage with Captain Shotover, there are echoes of the scenes of love and reconciliation between Lear and Cordelia in acts 4 and 5 of *King Lear*.

The character of King Lear is recalled in *Heartbreak House* in several different ways. Shakespeare's protagonist is most obviously echoed in the portrayal of Captain Shotover, in ways we have already observed. But Shaw creates a strange Shakespearean coupling by introducing equally strong recollections of Lear in the unlikely person of the *"entirely commonplace"* (86) Boss Mangan. Both Shotover and Mangan echo Lear's cry of "Howl, howl, howl, howl!" in the last scene of *King Lear*—Shotover with his *"strange wail in the darkness"* (104) as he rails at his daughters at the end of act 1, and Mangan with his "howling" in act 3.

Shaw allots to Mangan alone, however, two of the most specific reminiscences of Lear in the play. In acts 1 and 2 of *King Lear* Shakespeare gives Lear two premonitions of his own insanity. Near the end of act 1 he exclaims, "O! let me not be mad, not mad, sweet heaven" (1.5.43), and shortly afterwards, in act 2, he feels the swelling within him of *"hysterica passio"* (2.4.55), a disorder that had the curious alternative name in Elizabethan times of "the suffocation of the mother," because its symptoms included a choking in the throat that was popularly associated with the idea of suffocation in the womb.[26] Lear alludes to this alternative name when he says, "O! how this mother swells up toward my heart" (2.4.54). Mangan, the victim of coercive mothering in *Heartbreak House*, has a similar kind of frenzied apprehension of encroaching madness when he is being tormented by the brazen candor of Ellie Dunn in the opening scene of act 2. Like Lear, Mangan admits his need of feminine tenderness and love, but in doing so he makes himself vulnerable to cruelty and contempt: "MANGAN. (*clutching at his bursting temples*) Oh, this is a crazy house. Or else I'm going clean off my chump. . . . (*throwing himself into the chair distractedly*) My brain wont stand it. My head's going to split. Help! Help me to hold it. Quick: hold it: squeeze it. Save me" (112).

Anne Wright draws attention to the "unmistakeable [further] echo of *King Lear*" in act 3 of *Heartbreak House*, when Mangan begins to strip off his clothes, as does Lear during the storm on the heath. Wright believes this echo "points to the centrality of Mangan not only as a comic butt . . . but also as a potentially tragic figure and sacrificial victim" (Wright 1984, 99–100). Mangan is certainly victimized, but, as with so many other echoes in the play, the significance of the recollections of Lear in the portrayal of Mangan is defined as much by difference from, as resemblance to, the original. Mangan and Lear strip for very different reasons, and with very different dramatic effects. Lear is confronted on the heath by the naked Edgar, "unaccommodated man" (3.4.104–105), and wants to imitate his state. His action can be seen not only as a moment of empathy with suffering and degradation but

Pamela Rabe as Ellie Dunn and Alan Cassell as Boss Mangan in a scene from act 2 of *Heartbreak House*, Melbourne Theatre Company, Melbourne, Australia, 1986. *Photograph by David Parker. Used with kind permission of the Melbourne Theatre Company.*

also as an extremely powerful expression of his demotion in the play—his loss of kingly rank, dignity, and difference.

Mangan begins to strip off his clothes as a desperate and impotent gesture of protest at the cruel games of stripping away of masks and exposure of weaknesses at the playing of which the clever conversational duelists of Heartbreak House are such experts. It is a moment of bathos rather than pathos, and Hesione's maternal reproof (which contains another reminder of Lear's madness) extends an exquisitely comic moment: "Alfred: for shame! Are you mad?" (166). Mangan is not even remotely a figure of tragic stature, and the parodic echoes of Lear in Shaw's characterization serve rather to underline this—perhaps also to stir at the roots of our understanding of the tragic, as elsewhere the play questions conventional ideas of heartbreak. Mangan's portrayal can be seen to exemplify one of the many ways in which tragic experience undergoes a sea-change in *Heartbreak House*.

A further dimension of the intertextual connections of *Heartbreak House* with *King Lear* can be seen in the treatment of sexual relations. In *King Lear* Goneril comes to regard her recently acquired husband, Albany, as "milk-liver'd" and an overscrupulous "moral fool" (4.2.50, 58). Her assumption of domination over him is likened to the treatment of Hercules by Omphale in the classical legend, in which the great hero is reduced to effeminacy and set to work on the distaff by the woman he becomes enamored of in one of his journeys: "I must," says Goneril to Edmund, "change arms at home, and give the distaff / Into my husband's hands" (4.2.17–18).[27]

As we have seen, Hector is another husband reduced to abject subordination by a woman. He also resembles Albany in his capacity for moral idealism and compassion. It is fitting therefore that Shaw should have Hector almost quote the words, "Fall and cease," that Shakespeare gives to Albany at a moment of intense emotional crisis in the last scene of *King Lear* (5.3.263). In his exclamation Albany is calling on the heavens to fall and bring all things to an end, to bring about an apocalyptic moment. Hector, at the end of act 2 of *Heartbreak House*, in a moment of unbearable frustration at "women! women! women!," likewise calls on the heavens to "Fall and crush" (157). But, again, the echoes are far from straightforward, and difference matters as much as resemblance. Hesione wins dominance over Hector by much more subtle means than those employed by Goneril with Albany. Goneril's ferocious and overt attack on Albany's "manhood" is not at all recalled in Hesione's relation with Hector, which is, on the contrary, loving, solicitous, and affectionate. The resultant effects, of male subordination and emasculation, may be similar, but the means by which they are obtained are different. Shaw refines and sophisticates the Shakespearean portrayal of female cruelty and tyranny.

Discussion of the connections between *Heartbreak House* and the Russian works alluded to in the subtitle "A Fantasia in the Russian Manner on English Themes," and specifically cited in the Preface as earlier portraits of "Heartbreak House," has, understandably, tended to be concentrated on the relationship with Chekhov's *The Cherry Orchard*, a performance of which Shaw attended in May 1911.[28] There are, indeed, many significant links with *The Cherry Orchard* in *Heartbreak House*. The "feckless, unbusiness-like, queer people" (as Lopakhin calls them)[29] who make up Ranyevskaia's circle in *The Cherry Orchard* together represent a social order that has lost control of its destiny and is threatened by mainly self-induced destruction.

As in *Heartbreak House*, a sense of impending doom is increasingly felt as Chekhov's play develops. The cherry orchard and Heartbreak House are places under threat of annihilation. "I keep expecting something dreadful to happen . . . as if the house were going to fall down on us," says Ranyevskaia in act 2 of *The Cherry Orchard* (359). Similar expectations of catastrophe permeate act 3 of *Heartbreak House*, beginning with Mangan's presentiment of his death and Hesione's report of hearing a mysterious "splendid drumming in the sky" (159). In both plays the place evoked in the stage setting becomes explicitly a metaphor for a national social predicament: "The whole of Russia is our orchard" (CO, 367), says the idealistic student, Trofimov, in his outcry about the wasteful and useless lives of the orchard's indolent owners. And reference has already been made to Hector's speech in act 3 of *Heartbreak House*, in which the ship/house of the play's setting is metaphorically identified with England (177).

But many of the links between *Heartbreak House* and *The Cherry Orchard* display the same kind of *discordia concors* as those between Shaw's play and *King Lear*. Echoes of *The Cherry Orchard* are modified and Shavianized in *Heartbreak House* in such a way as to effect a complete transformation of the Chekhovian motifs. Shortly after the opening of Chekhov's play (following Lopakhin's report of his having fallen asleep over a book, which anticipates the first glimpse of Ellie Dunn in *Heartbreak House*) Ranyevskaia, returning home after a long absence, bursts onto the scene with joyous cries about the nursery, which brings back ecstatically happy memories of her childhood: "The nursery, my dear, my beautiful room! . . . I used to sleep here when I was little. . . . (*cries*) And now I feel as if I were little again" (*CO*, 336). Ariadne's entry shortly after the beginning of *Heartbreak House* conveys the impression of a theatrical quotation from Chekhov. She is also returning home after a long absence, and her first words in the play are addressed to the Nurse.

Shaw, however, has his character convey a much more astringent view of childhood and its associations than that expressed in Ranyevskaia's opening speeches. In place of the latter's tearfully joyous revisiting of the nursery and recognition of loved ones we have Ariadne, who thinks Ellie must be one of her nieces; who is not recognized by her own father; who rails against the disorder of the house, of which she has only unhappy memories; and, especially, who does not want to be accommodated in her childhood bedroom. When Shotover, still infuriatingly refusing to acknowledge that it is Ariadne he is addressing, proposes to her that she sleep in "Ariadne's old room," her indignant reply conveys feelings of deep animosity toward this room:

THE CAPTAIN. . . . You shall sleep in Ariadne's old room.

LADY UTTERWORD. Indeed I shall do nothing of the sort. That little hole! (72)

Hesione's report, early in act 3, of a "splendid drumming in the sky" (159) recalls, in several details, the episode in *The Cherry Orchard* where a sound, as of a string snapping, breaks a silence that has descended on the characters near the end of act 2. In each case the sound comes "*out of the sky*" (*CO*, 365) and from a distance, and then it dies away. In each case there is speculation about the source of the sound (with the two prosaic men, Lopakhin and Mangan, giving similarly commonsensical explanations) followed by discussion about what the sound might signify. Here again, however, Shaw gives this Chekhovian echo distinct inflections, which have the effect of radically adjusting the meaning of the original. Chekhov clearly wanted the strange sound in his play to convey a mood of almost indescribable sadness: the stage direction calls for the sound to fade in a melancholy diminuendo, "*slowly and sadly dying away*" (CO, 365). A quite different impression about the distant sound in the sky is created in *Heartbreak House*. Hesione's description of the sound as "a sort of splendid drumming in the sky" (159) conveys a sense of excitement and exhilaration. When the sound returns at the end of the play she again calls it "splendid" and says that it is "like Beethoven," a comparison underlined in Ellie's response, "By thunder, Hesione: it is Beethoven" (178). The exquisite sadness and foreboding that surrounds the snapping of the string in Chekhov's play is replaced by a mood of fierce exuberance in *Heartbreak House*.

Shaw also diverges from his Russian model when the characters discuss the possible significance of the sound. In the open country scene of act 2 of *The Cherry Orchard* the mysterious sound elicits from Ranyevskaia a shudder and a vague sense of uneasiness: "It sounded unpleasant, somehow" (CO, 365). After another pause in conversation, the old servant, Feers, calls to mind similar ominous sounds heard in the reign of Czar Alexander II, before the emancipation of the serfs, which he ironically refers to as "the misfortune" (CO, 365). Feers's speech provides a hint that another profound change in the social order of Russia may be heralded by this sound. But in the garden scene of act 3 of *Heartbreak House* the sound is specifically related, in a speech by Hector, to the possibility of an apocalyptic moment in human history, a divine intervention and punishment. The sound is "heaven's threatening growl of disgust at us useless futile creatures. . . . Either out of that darkness some new creation will come to supplant us as we have supplanted the animals, or the heavens will fall in thunder and destroy us" (159).

Of the two other Chekhov portraits of houses of heartbreak Shaw refers to in his Preface, *The Seagull* and *Uncle Vanya*, it is the latter that has the closer links with *Heartbreak House*. *Uncle Vanya* was performed in London by the Stage Society, at Shaw's urging, in 1914. The household of the aged and irritable Professor Serebriakov in *Uncle Vanya* is a place in which, as we are told by his charming and attractive young wife, Yeliena, "things have gone to pieces."[30] Like the abode of Shotover, that of Serebriakov is one of disorder and heartbreak. The main occupation of the characters in this suffocating[31] hothouse is their indulgence in fruitless and destructive amatory negotiations like those in *Heartbreak House*.

At the center of these negotiations is the sexually magnetic Yeliena, who is hopelessly courted by both Uncle Vanya and the frequently visiting Doctor Astrov. Yeliena, who one English theater critic has described as "a Russian Hedda Gabler,"[32] has much in common also with the dangerously attractive daughters of the Shotover household. Referring to the way in which Yeliena distracts Astrov from his practice and his forestry, her stepdaughter, Sonia, declares, "You must be a witch" (*UV*, 218), and Astrov describes her as "a charming bird of prey," before saying to her, in complete submission to her powers, "Here I am, devour me" (*UV*, 224). (Shaw can hardly have failed to be reminded by this dramatic moment in *Uncle Vanya* of his own Ann Whitefield in *Man and Superman*, who, as Jack Tanner claims, in an admonitory speech to Octavius, gobbles up her male prey like a boa constrictor.)[33]

A view of Chekhov as philosophically and politically uncommitted, as a humane and compassionate fatalist who makes no judgments about his characters, is strongly entrenched in the critical tradition surrounding his work. But such a view is particularly difficult to sustain in the cases of *The Cherry Orchard* and *Uncle Vanya*.[34] Despite the complexities of characterization and action and the more than occasional glimpses into metaphysical voids of absurdity, these plays contain powerful and incisive critiques of contemporary society. The landowning class is portrayed as idle, selfish, and feckless. The intellectuals of Chekhov's Russia are hopelessly ineffectual and remote from issues that concern the commonweal. Near the end of *The Cherry Orchard*, great concern is expressed about the failing health of the old, loyal servant, Feers. Within a few minutes' playing time, however, Feers is simply forgotten by his employers and is left alone onstage to make his sad closing soliloquy. The Ranyevskaia party, having visited the estate like a flock of birds to feed on memories, abruptly and insouciantly departs, apparently without any further thought for the major human problem left behind.

Serebriakov, the retired professor and owner of the estate on which *Uncle Vanya* is set, is presented as a monster of self-engrossment and hypochondriacal irritability who "for twenty five years has been chewing over other people's ideas about realism, naturalism and all that sort of nonsense" (*UV*, 191). Astrov, the play's man of action and vision, talks of an intellectual class that is "positively rotten with intro-spection and futile cerebration"; he sees around him in the district "a picture of decay . . . caused by inertia, by ignorance, by utter irrespon-sibility" (*UV*, 211, 223).

Shaw was justified in seeing Chekhov's portrayals of social decay and helpless irresponsibility in Russia as precursors of his own presen-tation, in *Heartbreak House*, of a cultivated intelligentsia that has lost control of its destiny and plays dangerous and foolish games of love as civilization drifts toward self-destruction. In Shaw's play, however, the auguries of doom are much more strongly stressed. The sad music of the snapped string gives way to tumultuous drumming and explosion, as well as to intimations of the possible demise not simply of a social order but of civilization itself.

By the time he came to write the Preface to *Heartbreak House* for publication in 1919, the play had clearly become, in Shaw's pub-licly presented account of it, a dramatized treatise about a critical moment in human history. The Preface, of course, gives no hint of the personal experiences Shaw was drawing on in the play, and it gives very little idea of the depth and complexity of the play's literary rela-tions. Although it is a powerful essay and has clear validity as an account of the social themes of the play, the Preface bears a distinctly ironic relationship to some of the less philosophical matters involved in the genesis of *Heartbreak House*. In extreme reaction to late nine-teenth-century notions of *l'art pour l'art*, Shaw rejoiced in carrying out regular demolitions of his "literary" reputation as a dramatist by insist-ing, in the superbly written prefaces, that his plays are strictly to be regarded as sociological essays, cast in dramatic form, and designed for the instruction and improvement of the human race, especially for those members living in the southern counties of England. Analysis of the play as a chamber of personal and literary echoes does not deny the strength of its social critique, but it does show *Heartbreak House* to be at once a more autobiographical and more typically modernist play than might otherwise be apparent.

Helen Westley as Nurse Guinness in *Heartbreak House*, Garrick Theater, New York, 1920. *Photograph by Ira D. Schwarz. Used by permission of the British Library.*

5

Discontinuities

Discontinuity is everywhere apparent in the dramatic form and characterization of *Heartbreak House*. Some sense of a steadily evolving, and resolved, dramatic narrative is supplied by the story of Ellie's progress through the play. Her unfolding story—passing through the phases of heartbreak about "Marcus Darnley," the bargaining with and rejection of Mangan, to the announcement of her spiritual marriage with Captain Shotover—gives the play a vertebral structure. But alongside this story Shaw generates numerous subsidiary narratives that typically end either in nothing—such as Hesione's flirtation with Mazzini Dunn—or in various forms of frustrated desire.

The action of *Heartbreak House* develops in a series of fitful meetings, flirtations, discussions, and games of exposure that are generally inconsequential (except in negative ways) but collectively add up to a powerful portrait and critique of a society on the brink of self-destruction. The play's subtitle, "A Fantasia," referring to musical compositions that are not tied to strict or regular form (such as that of the fugue) but instead comprise a series of freely arranged improvizations, provides an apt analogy to the structure of the play.[1] As Nurse Guinness remarks very early in the play (telling the audience, as well as

Ellie Dunn, what to expect), *Heartbreak House* is "full of surprises" (62). The irregular organization of the play contributes to a sense of disconcerting strangeness and quirkiness in its atmosphere, which has prompted comparisons with works such as Strindberg's *A Dream Play* and Lewis Carroll's *Alice in Wonderland*.[2] Ellie Dunn's description of the house in the act 3 speech in which she gives it its name encapsulates a principle of conflicting perspectives that can be seen at work in the whole artistic design of *Heartbreak House*: "This silly house, this strangely happy house, this agonising house, this house without foundations. I shall call it Heartbreak House" (171).

The dramaturgical design of the play is extraordinarily complex. With 10 characters, all of whom have important roles, and a comparatively slight thread of main plot, Shaw set himself a difficult task of composition. The play is characterized by alternating periods of restless activity, involving varying numbers of characters, with intense "duets," such as those between Ellie and Hesione in act 1, and "trios" such as that between Mangan, Ellie, and Hesione in act 2. The first act of *Heartbreak House* is one of the most brilliantly orchestrated expositional movements in English comedy. While Captain Shotover, appearing and disappearing like a figure on a marionette clock, diverts us with his eccentric views and provocative confusions of identity, the entire cast, except for the Burglar, is introduced and the principal dramatic situation established. The act contains more than 60 entrances and exits, but there is no sense of strained contrivance in these stage movements. Shaw took playwright Arthur Wing Pinero to task for the creaking stage device in act 1 of *The Second Mrs. Tanqueray*, when Aubrey steps aside to write some letters so that other characters can conduct a conversation about him (*Theatres*, 1:45). No such awkwardness is apparent in the "half-procession, half-pandemonium" of *Heartbreak House*.

The main activities in Heartbreak House are the playing of games of flirtation and struggles for power between the sexes, in which the women of the house are almost uniformly victorious. A sinister, unstable, and ruthless outside world of big business is strongly evoked in the stories of Mangan and Mazzini Dunn. Captain Shotover's stockpile of dynamite and inventions of terrible weapons of destruction—

the economic underpinning of the house—supply further images of an outside world full of threat and violence. But the foreground of the play's numerous spheres of interest is occupied by the encounters of various kinds between the sexes.

Ellie Dunn's act 1 account of her romance with "Marcus Darnley" is the first of a series of dramatic narratives about relations between the sexes that typically have disappointing and frustrating conclusions. In act 2 Ellie embarks on her cynical negotiations with Mangan for a marriage of convenience. In the course of this laying of cards on the table, Ellie and Mangan reveal that their basic design in such a relationship would be to enable the continuation of their interests in Hector, in Ellie's case, and Hesione in Mangan's. Her act 3 announcement of her spiritual marriage to Captain Shotover, during the speaking of which the Captain remains fast asleep, is comically at odds with all conventions of romance, even though it does provide some resolution of her fortunes. Only in the highly charged last minutes of act 3 is the idea of romance revived, when Ellie reverts to Hector's pseudonym, "Marcus." But here the context creates a powerful irony. It is when Hector is behaving in a quite suicidal fashion by wanting to turn on all the lights in the house that Shaw has Ellie say, "(*tense with excitement*) Set fire to the house, Marcus" (179). The mingled suggestions in this speech of romance and death-wish bring the play into momentary contact with works such as Wagner's *Tristan and Isolde*,[3] which climax in a *liebestod*.

The other encounters in the play's complex dance of uncompleted relations are those of Hector with Ariadne, Hesione with Mangan and Mazzini Dunn, and Ariadne with Randall. Most of these encounters resemble cruel games played by children. Hesione, the "siren . . . born to lead men by the nose" (122), deliberately sets out to "fascinate" (99) Mangan so as to divert his attention from Ellie. As Hesione mischievously leads Mangan out for a walk on the heath under the moon in act 2, he goes out seduced but writhing and sobbing (140). She has Mangan completely in her thrall, and she uses tenderness toward him in a quite destructive way. Hesione also brings Mazzini Dunn to tears before her unreciprocated flirtation with him earlier in act 2 (119).

The stage direction describing Hector's first reaction to Ariadne makes him sound rather like a dog that has found a prospective mate: "*looking at her with a piercing glance . . . his moustache bristling*" (92). Hector is physically magnetized by Ariadne but at the same cordially detests her, and twice he threatens to kill her (99, 155). This is another one of the play's twisted, tormenting, and unfulfilled relationships. The childish quality of the "cat and mouse game[s] with the other sex" (155) played in *Heartbreak House* is emphasized by Hector's question to Randall, "Why should you let yourself be dragged about and beaten by Ariadne as a toy donkey is dragged about and beaten by a child?" (156). With comical hauteur, Ariadne refuses to waste a single word of sympathy on her wretched slave, Randall, who is still trying to carry out her bidding by playing "Keep the Home Fires Burning" on his flute as the play ends.

As Weintraub and Wright point out in their introduction to the facsimile of the typescript of *Heartbreak House*, Shaw originally included in the play some fairly clear indications that the relationship of Ariadne and Randall was that of lovers, in the sexual sense. In the early draft of the play Hesione arranges for Randall's bedroom to be next door to Ariadne's and refers to him as her sister's "young man" (Weintraub and Wright, xxi, 51, 55). Shaw subsequently removed these innuendoes, however, and it is doubtful in the play as to whether Ariadne has ever granted Randall sexual favors. His (possibly unreliable) answer to Hector's direct question, "Are you her lover?" is that he is so "in a Platonic sense" (156). The changes Shaw made in the depiction of their relationship further bring out the teasing quality of Ariadne's treatment of Randall.

Heartbreak House is a "house without foundations" (171), in which instability is a reigning principle. The "nightmarish fluidity" of the characterization provides an example of Shaw's deliberately destabilizing strategies. From early in act 1 a pattern of playful uncertainty about identity and moral character is created. Ellie is mistakenly thought by Ariadne to be one of her nieces. Ariadne is not recognized as herself by either Captain Shotover or Hesione. Mazzini Dunn is insultingly confused by Shotover with another person called Dunn, the alleged drunken pirate, thief, and murderer who formerly served as his boatswain and who turns up as the Burglar in act 2. When Randall, the last of the characters to arrive in act 1, politely says to Shotover, "I'm afraid you dont know who I am," the Captain denies any interest in discriminations between individual specimens of the human race: "Do you suppose that at my age I make distinctions between one fellow-creature and another?" (90).

Comic confusion between the two Dunns—the "drinking Dunn" and the "thinking Dunn" (137)—is a sustained motif, which raises puzzling questions about the character and thematic significance of the Mazzini Dunn side of this equation. The contrast between his courteous, tactful, and harmless demeanor, as suggested in the dialogues in which he is engaged, and the aspersions cast on him by Captain Shotover is extreme. Captain Shotover's confusion of the two Dunns may be dismissed by Hesione as one of her father's "mad as a hatter" (72) eccentricities,[4] but the play invites reflection at deeper levels on the connections between Mazzini Dunn and the other two "burglars," Billy Dunn and Mangan.

Mazzini Dunn describes himself to Hesione in act 2 as "a consecrated soldier of freedom" (115). This underlines the connection Shaw evidently intended to establish with Giuseppe Mazzini (1805–72), the leader of a revolutionary republican movement in nineteenth-century Italy that sought to free the various Italian states from domination by foreign powers. From the late 1830s, Mazzini had several periods of residence in London, and his name would have been well known to English radicals in Shaw's early days with the Fabian Society. His political activities were largely unsuccessful, but he was an influential figure in nineteenth-century Italian struggles for independence. His English connections were mostly with the Liberals, and this could well be part of the explanation for Shaw's rather satirical treatment of Mazzini Dunn.

For all his charm, courtesy, and love of Shakespeare, Mazzini is shown in the play to be completely in the grip of the capitalist system of exploitation to which Mangan belongs. He is a factotum in the hoggish world of big business, which is conjured up in the play as part of the enemy that needs to be destroyed. Mazzini Dunn's fantastic, Shotover-created other self as pirate, thief and murderer becomes more explicable when the character is seen in the allegorical perspective his historically related name brings into play. In this perspective Mazzini is part of the failed nineteenth-century tradition of liberalism that accommodated itself to the prevailing systems of capitalism while presenting itself as a party whose main rationale was the preservation of liberty and individual freedom. Mazzini's Young Italy nationalistic movement was a model for the Young Ireland movement for which the poet James Clarence Mangan was a major spokesman.[5] The satirical thrust of bringing together the names of two ardent nationalists of Italy and Ireland as fictional participants in shady capitalistic enterprise could hardly have been lost on at least some of the early readers and audiences of *Heartbreak House.*

The double vision with which the play invites us to see Mazzini is reflected in various other ways in which characters are portrayed. As a group, the characters assembled in *Heartbreak House* are shown in an ambiguous, contradictory light. When, in act 3, Hector dubs the house's inhabitants "heartbroken imbeciles" (173), Mazzini Dunn replies, "Oh no. Surely, if I may so, rather a favourable specimen of what is best in our English culture. You are very charming people, most advanced, unprejudiced, frank, humane, unconventional, democratic, free-thinking, and everything that is delightful to thoughtful people" (173).

This extremely charitable, and rather bland, view of the wastrels of Heartbreak House as "very charming people" is, of course, charged with irony. Dunn's rose-colored spectacles here obscure from view the cruel, childish games of exposure and torment that so much of the play depicts. Yet this summary description of the characters is not by any means entirely contradicted by their portrayal in the rest of the play. Whatever else they may be, the characters are not representative of dull middle-class virtues. Terms such as "advanced," "unprejudiced," "frank," "free-thinking," and so forth could very well be applied not only to a large section of Shaw's own social and intellectual circle but also to the staple audiences of his plays at the Court Theatre and elsewhere in the early years of the twentieth century. Dunn's speech, then, can be seen as a sudden holding up of a mirror to, and confrontation of, the English intelligentsia, and as making a sardonic, satirical attack on its collective self-image. In effect, the speech establishes an uncomfortable affinity between the charming, intelligent, and liberal-minded wasters and destroyers onstage, facing the doom of apocalypse, and the charming and intelligent people sitting in the audience.

Individually, most of the characters display the same protean qualities. Their handling by Shaw is reminiscent of D. H. Lawrence's remark, apropos his novel *The Rainbow*, about his methods of characterization: "You mustn't look in my novel for the old stable ego of the character." Lawrence goes on to speak of "another ego" that, while remaining a basically unchanged element, passes through various "allotropic states."[6] The characters in *Heartbreak House* can be seen to answer to this Lawrentian concept of the ego. Thus, for example, Ellie Dunn develops from the ingenue figure of act 1 to the callous negotiator of act 2 to the discoverer of the importance of "life with a blessing" (169) in act 3. Shotover is presented in different lights as shrewd sage and critic on the one hand and destructive and callous old man, a *senex irascibilis*, on the other.

Hesione, the most mercurial character, is portrayed as being by turns beguiling, witty, affectionate, solicitous, mischievous, cruel, designing, manipulative, and dangerous. It is symbolic of the deliberate ambiguity with which Shaw presents Hesione that the question raised in act 2 as to whether her magnificent black hair is her own or not is never completely resolved. In her act 2 dialogue with Ellie Hesione hints that "perhaps it comes off at night" (125), but her subsequent challenge to Ellie to try pulling the hair creates further mystification. The subject returns in a speech by Ellie in act 3, which openly reflects on the unreliability, the shifting-sands quality, of the play's narratological "evidence":

> ELLIE. There seems to be nothing real in the world except my father and Shakespear. Marcus's tigers are false; Mr Mangan's millions are false; there is nothing really strong and true about Hesione but her beautiful black hair; and Lady Utterword is too pretty to be real. The one thing that was left to me was the Captain's seventh degree of concentration; and that turns out to be—
>
> CAPTAIN SHOTOVER. Rum. (165–66)

In the stage direction that introduces Boss Mangan in act 1, his features are described as *"entirely commonplace,"* and in some ways his character matches this description. But on closer inspection he too turns out to be a very complex dramatic creation. In a sense there are two Mangans in the play, echoing the double image of Dunn. One construction of Mangan, largely but not exclusively created in the dialogue of other characters, is that of the ruthless, exploitative capitalist boss, a thoroughly disagreeable hog of business. Fierce odium is directed at him by Captain Shotover, who greets him in a very hostile fashion and later tells Hector that the purpose of his dynamite is "to kill fellows like Mangan." Mangan is lumped together by the Captain with "these hogs to whom the universe is nothing but a machine for greasing their bristles and filling their snouts" (100). Mangan is similarly depersonalized and treated with contempt by Ellie and Hesione as he listens helplessly to their insults in the hypnotized trance into which Ellie has induced in him in act 2. During this scene he is twice referred to as an "object," and Ellie callously remarks that "if Mangan has nothing else he has money" (123, 124).

But there are several ways in which these repellent images of Mangan are modified. When he is woken from his trance in the scene just referred to, important changes occur in the presentation of his character. We learn that he has another first name as well as the depersonalizing one of "Boss." He is called Alfred, a name Hesione playfully converts to "Little Alf!" as she surveys him, saying, "It comes to me suddenly that you are a real person: that you had a mother, like anyone else" (129). In this scene it is not only discovered that he is a "real person" but also that he has a heart capable of being wounded. Reduced to tears over Hesione's duplicitous behavior toward him, he scores a considerable moral victory over her at this point.

Mangan's vulnerability, his desperate clutchings for sanity and self-respect, and his comical, exasperated protests at the behavior of people in Heartbreak House ("The very burglars cant behave naturally in this house" [134]) all tend to modify the picture of him as merely the ruthless, exploitative tycoon. What he *is* as "Alfred" and what he *symbolizes* as "Boss" Mangan become distinguishable fictional constructions in the play. The text certainly leaves room for an actor to present Mangan as, in Mazzini Dunn's words, "quite a good fellow in his way" (118), and sympathetic portrayals of the character are not uncommon. A reviewer of a 1959 Royal Academy of Dramatic Art production of the play described "a North country Mangan so human as almost to condemn Shaw's estimate of the character."[7]

Instability and change are also reigning principles in the generic affiliations of *Heartbreak House*. The play belongs, fundamentally, to the nineteenth-century and early modern tradition of naturalism. House party gatherings of the kind presented in the play were common enough both in life and fiction of the Edwardian period, and both setting and characterization in *Heartbreak House* basically conform to naturalist conventions. But the play presses at the limits of these conventions and often breaks free from them altogether, in a number of different ways. Ellie's act 1 account of her affair with "Marcus Darnley," the hero of unknown origins found as a baby in "an antique chest, one summer morning in a rose garden, after a night of the most terrible thunderstorm" (81), plunges the play briefly into a world of romantic fantasy. In the middle of the play, with the introduction of the eccentric Burglar, we are in the realm of farce. At the end of of act 1 Shaw momentarily abandons naturalism altogether when he has Shotover, Hesione, and Hector break into a weird chant on the darkened stage about the Shotover household. Here, and in the final scene of the play, Shaw moves in the direction of expressionist drama.

Several other features of *Heartbreak House* tend to push it to the very limits, and beyond, of naturalism. As the play develops, the ship-like setting and the numerous maritime images in the dialogue create multifaceted metaphors of both public and private predicaments. Stage lighting and the numerous references to darkness and light in the dialogue also have metaphorical significance. Shotover's alleged dabbling in the past with black magic in Zanzibar and his strange quest for the seventh degree of concentration and supernatural powers of destruction, the demonic qualities of the Shotover daughters, and the mysterious, unspecified forces of violence unleashed at the play's end are among other factors that take the play outside the bounds of naturalistic *vraisemblance*.

6

"Out of That Darkness":
Symbolism and the Supernatural

The departures from strictly naturalistic theatrical values that occur in *Heartbreak House* can be traced in several different areas of dramatic composition. Symbolic uses of the play's shiplike setting, lighting effects, costume, and even the color of hair specified for some of the characters combine with imagery, characterization, and narratives to push the work in the direction of expressionist fantasy and parable. The play also conjures up images of supernatural forces and demonic creatures, of possible divine intervention in human history, and of mystical experience, which also work against its simple classification as an example of naturalist theater.

In the great majority of run-of-the-mill naturalist plays of the early modern period, the settings remain, in semiotic terms, largely inert. They are a backdrop to the action, with no particular significance except to convey the notion that the fictional world onstage and the "real" world outside the theater are closely related. When the curtain went up at the first production of *The Second Mrs. Tanqueray* in 1893, well-to-do members of the audience saw a drawing room that, for many, was exactly the kind of drawing room they had just left to come to the theater. For less well-to-do members of the audience the room most likely created an image of desirable luxury, much in the way as magazines such as *Vogue Living* function today. But the Victorian furniture and ornament specified in the stage directions never acquires any really significant meaning in the play, except to locate it in a certain social context.

In the hands of such playwrights as Ibsen, Strindberg, Chekhov, and Shaw, however, naturalistic settings and other nonverbal devices can acquire powerful symbolic dimensions of meaning. Ibsen's wonderfully imagined doll's house becomes a cage of constriction, a place of threatening spaces and doors from which the socially constructed child-bride and fluttering bird, Nora, finally resolves to escape. The Captain's study in Strindberg's *The Father* is another place of constraint and oppression, and the kitchen in *Miss Julie* represents a social divide that his heroine has dangerously crossed. Chekhov's cherry orchard projects complex symbols of private nostalgia and desire, as well as larger social problems, as his apparently rambling but amazingly taut play unfolds.

In *Heartbreak House* the shiplike dwelling of Shotover combines with various maritime images in the dialogue to create a multifaceted symbolic pattern. The curtain first rises on the scene of a room *"built so as to resemble the after part of an old-fashioned high pooped ship"* (59). Although this is an unusual setting, nothing in it transgresses the bounds of naturalism. By the end of the play, however, the house has become symbolically equated with the whole condition of a society. The ship-house of Shotover and the state of England become imaginatively fused in the final scene in a number of ways, most obviously in Hector's questions: "And this ship that we are all in? This soul's prison we call England" (177). The "ship" is embarked on a dangerous, apparently rudderless and unnavigated voyage in history—a voyage with a calamitous wreck as its possible conclusion. Whereas at the beginning of the play the setting may seem no more than a whimsical piece of interior domestic design, creating opportunities for various jokes and the device of Shotover's occasional blasts on his Captain's whistle, by the end it has become a powerful symbol of national destiny.

A significant feature of the setting of *Heartbreak House* is that it is not a conceptually static place. As I point out in Chapter 4, the ship-like houses of nineteenth-century fiction are safe, dry havens on land. Their captains have come to harbor. By contrast, Shaw's creation in his play of the sense that this ship-house is actually involved in a perilous voyage gives the play's setting a remarkably dynamic quality. An adjoining symbolic "house"—that of the Church—has already foundered, through a failure of navigation, which Shotover sardonically draws attention to when news of the destruction of the rectory is reported in act 3: "CAPTAIN SHOTOVER. The Church is on the rocks, breaking up. I told him [the rector] it would unless it headed for God's open sea" (177–78). The Shotover ship-house is continually a site of danger and potential disaster. A half-comic hint of such danger is conveyed at the beginning of the play by the inclusion in the stage props of "a ship's fire bucket" (60)—a motif that anticipates the idea of a possible final conflagration as expressed in Ellie's excited command in the final scene of act 3, "Set fire to the house, Marcus" (179). The edge of danger is sharpened in act 1 when Captain Shotover returns from his gravel pit with some sticks of dynamite in his hand, which Hesione affectionately asks her "Daddiest" not to drop about the house (99). Captain Shotover's dynamite itself can be seen to have metaphorical value, as an expression of his destructive, finally impotent, animus toward the system represented by Mangan. Such literal intimations of danger have an obvious symbolic bearing on the play's portrayal of society.

The inhabitants of Heartbreak House are living on the edge of disaster, but it is only Hector and Shotover who show a full consciousness of the predicament the characters and their society are in—and even in this Shotover is Hector's mentor. The other characters preoccupy themselves with their games of sexual pursuit and exploitation, showing no awareness of the potentially catastrophic larger game of history in which they are caught up. Ariadne has firm views about the value of horses and stables, Empire and strict gubernatorial rule, and so can be said to have some knowledge of the political and social world "outside." Ellie gains insights about heartbreak, about the limitations of materialism, and about her own real ambitions. Mazzini

Dunn thinks nothing will happen. Mangan and Randall are the major sufferers from the games. It is Shotover, in his seafarer's images of deceptive calm before disaster, who supplies the principal articulation of the play's imaginative projection of doom. When Mazzini concludes a speech with "nothing happens," Shotover responds,

> At sea nothing happens to the sea. Nothing happens to the sky. The sun comes up from the east and goes down to the west. The moon grows from a sickle to an arc lamp, and comes later and later until she is lost in the light as other things are lost in the darkness. After the typhoon, the flying-fish glitter in the sunshine like birds. It's amazing how they get along, all things considered. Nothing happens, except something not worth mentioning.
>
> ELLIE. What is that, O Captain, my captain?
>
> CAPTAIN SHOTOVER. (*savagely*) Nothing but the smash of the drunken skipper's ship on the rocks, the splintering of her rotten timbers, the tearing of her rusty plates, the drowning of the crew like rats in a trap. (176)

Maritime imagery is also deployed by Shaw in other areas of the play's thematic concerns. Especially important here is the way in which such imagery is drawn into the treatment of the theme of heartbreak. Heartbreak is usually thought of as a state of overwhelming sorrow and grief, a kind of psychic collapse, or total loss of morale and happiness brought about by some suffering such as rejection in love or unbearable loss. Although the play continually suggests an abundance of heartbreaking situations in the lives of the characters, the mainly comic mode of the dramatic present stands in the way of sentimental expression of the experience of heartbreak. Randall and Mangan are comical in their abjection.

Ellie Dunn's immediate reaction to her discovery of the truth about "Marcus Darnley" is not one of tearful misery or despair but of anger. Shaw's handling of this moment is a parody of typical Victorian scenes of women fainting away on sofas and requiring smelling salts at the hearing of some devastating news. When Hector departs after the

Irene Worth as Hesione Hushabye and Sarah Badel as Ellie Dunn in
Heartbreak House, Lyric Theatre, London, 1967. *Photograph by Zoë
Dominic. Used with kind permission of Dominic Photography, London.*

revelation of his masquerade in act 1, Hesione arranges Ellie on the sofa and invites her to "have a good cry." But Ellie's response is to raise her head and say "damn," before castigating herself for her folly in being taken in by Hector's imposture (84). Several subsequent passages indicate that Ellie has indeed experienced heartbreak in the shattering of her illusions about Marcus Darnley. In her scene with Hesione in act 2 she declares that although she is not going to die of heartbreak, her heart is "broken, all the same"; and she alludes again to her heartbroken state in her later dialogue with Shotover in the same act (126, 148).

In the complex development of this theme in relation to Ellie, however, heartbreak is ultimately seen not as a negative state but as a release from the bondage of desire—a painful stage on the path to tranquility. Again, at this critical thematic locus a maritime metaphor is employed, as Ellie pronounces on Mangan's heartbreak: "(*in a strangely calm voice, staring into an imaginary distance*) His heart is breaking: that is all. . . . It is a curious sensation: the sort of pain that goes mercifully beyond our powers of feeling. When your heart is broken, your boats are burned: nothing matters any more. It is the end of happiness and the beginning of peace" (140). The escape from desire and hope that lies beyond heartbreak, the removal of the goals of happiness and security that come about when "your boats are burned," is seen by Ellie as creating for her new and unlimited powers of achievement:

> CAPTAIN SHOTOVER. Heartbreak? Are you one of those who are so sufficient to themselves that they are only happy when they are stripped of everything, even of hope?
>
> ELLIE. . . . It seems so; for I feel now as if there was nothing I could not do, because I want nothing.
>
> CAPTAIN SHOTOVER. Thats the only real strength. Thats genius. Thats better than rum. (148–49)

The scene that supplies this perspective on the theme of heartbreak begins with Ellie contemplatively standing sentry over Captain

Shotover working at his drawing board. From Shotover's first speech in the scene—a terse joke about the stormy quality of life in his house—images of seafaring are a constant refrain in the dialogue, and they serve the important function of helping to define the Shotover "philosophy." Captain Shotover is one of many Shaw characters who give expression to the idea that being fully and intensely alive involves danger and exposure to risk. Shaw was an audacious risk-taker, and many of the most dynamic of his dramatic creations share this characteristic. The author of the play-within-the play in Shaw's 1911 comedy, *Fanny's First Play*, belongs to a Cambridge Fabian Society with an unusual motto, "The ice of life is slippery" (3:368). Living out this philosophy, the heroine of Fanny's provocative play, Margaret Knox, a rebellious daughter of a kindly and bewildered bourgeois couple, breaks away from the family and deliberately courts danger by getting in trouble with the police. In *Misalliance* (1910) the Polish acrobat Lina Szczepanowska declares that "you cant live without running risks" (*Misalliance*, 194), having already spectacularly demonstrated her belief when she arrives at the Tarleton household with a miraculous acrobatic feat, as the airplane, piloted by her temporary boyfriend Percival, crashes into the family greenhouse. Two of Shaw's better-known heroines, Major Barbara and Saint Joan, are conspicuously daring in their pursuit of life aims that involve radical transgression of social expectations and conventions.

Shotover is the most articulate of all the advocates of living dangerously in Shaw's plays. He was 10 times happier than the younger generation, he tells Ellie, when he was on the bridge in a typhoon, or frozen in Arctic ice for "months in darkness": "At your age I looked for hardship, danger, horror, and death, that I might feel the life in me more intensely. I did not let the fear of death govern my life; and my reward was, I had my life" (146). Shotover's words in this scene help to provide an explanatory conceptual context for some aspects of the end of *Heartbreak House*, especially Hector's deliberate courting of danger by turning on all the lights and Ellie's wild encouragement of him to set fire to the house. The Beethoven music of the bombers represents simultaneously a moment of extreme danger and intense life.

"Out of That Darkness": Symbolism and the Supernatural

Images of darkness and light are frequently recurring motifs in the imaginative world of *Heartbreak House,* and they too contribute to the play's symbolic patterns. Negritude, black magic, and mysterious compacts in the past with forces of darkness are evoked as part of Shotover's background and also as part of the metaphysical world with which Ellie Dunn has to come to terms on her journey toward her spiritual marriage with Shotover. The presentation of Shotover's past is typical of the uncertain way in which narratological "evidence" is delivered. Early in act 1 Nurse Guinness tells Ellie that "they say he sold himself to the devil in Zanzibar before he was a captain; and the older he grows the more I believe them" (64). The details of this Faustian compact in the former British protectorate of Zanzibar in East Africa are never fully revealed, but the story is repeated later in the play in different recountings by the Burglar, Hector, and Shotover himself. The Burglar is convinced of the Captain's preternatural powers as water diviner, gold detector, exploder of cartridges in people's pockets with a glance of the eye, and finder-out of the secrets in "the heart of man" (137).

Hector—who at one point refers to Shotover as "that supernatural old man" (96)—also appears to accept the story of Shotover's pact with the devil, adding to the tale the statement that the devil gave Shotover "a black witch for a wife" and that the two demon daughters of Shotover are the "mystical progeny" of that union (156). Shotover himself recounts these stories in a different way, saying to Ellie that the story of his pact with the devil was a piece of trickery he used to force into submission the degraded men he had to deal with in his seafaring days (144–45). Earlier in the play he advises Mangan to marry a West Indian negress, saying that they make excellent wives, and that he himself was married to one for two years (89).

Despite his demystifying remarks, however, there remains a strong sense of Shotover's association with dark, supernatural forces. The ultimate quest of his inventiveness, according to Hector, is to discover "a psychic ray that will explode all the explosives at the will of a Mahatma" (95). The use of the term "Mahatma" here suggests a possible link, in the characterization of Shotover, with theosophical ideas. (When his Fabian friend Annie Besant deserted the cause to become a

Cedric Hardwicke as Captain Shotover, *Heartbreak House*, Queen's Theatre, London, 1932. *Photograph by Pollard Crowther from the collections of the Theatre Museum, London. Used by permission of the Board of Trustees of the Victoria and Albert Museum.*

convert to Theosophy, Shaw is alleged to have said that she had no need to go to Tibet to find a Mahatma as he himself was perfectly capable of fulfilling the role: "Here and now is your Mahatma. I am your Mahatma.")[1] In Theosophy, a religio-philosophical system promoted in Shaw's lifetime by, among others, the celebrated Madame Blavatsky—a Mahatma is a type of guru, endowed with supernatural powers.

According to the esoteric Eastern religious teachings Madame Blavatsky expounded in *The Secret Doctrine*, a book that came into Shaw's hands in 1889, there are seven paths to the blissful state of Nirvana, when the individual ceases to exist and becomes identified with the divine essence.[2] Primeval entities of intelligence are seen as passing through seven phases (of which one is the human) in which there is a progressive apprehension of reality and stripping away of illusion on the path toward "the absolute consciousness":

> As we rise in the scale of development we perceive that during the stages through which we have passed we mistook shadows for realities, and the upward progress of the Ego is a series of progressive awakenings, each advance bringing with it the idea that now, at last, we have reached "reality"; but only when we shall have reached the absolute Consciousness, and blended our own with it, shall we be free from the delusions produced by Maya [illusion].[3]

The motif in *Heartbreak House* of Shotover's striving to reach the "seventh degree of concentration" has the appearance of a parodic and comic version of the mystical path described in Madame Blavatsky's work. (The topic was further developed in the fantasy of the preternaturally evolved intelligences of the He-Ancient and the She-Ancient in the work Shaw wrote immediately after *Heartbreak House, Back to Methuselah*.) But in Shaw's creation of the Shotover persona there is an ironic relation with the fundamentally benign, if at times hopelessly opaque, system of ideas Blavatsky and her followers were espousing. In *The Secret Doctrine* reference is made to the idea that the Brahma, or Supreme Being, is "constantly moved by the desire to create"

(Blavatsky, 107). In Shaw's play, however, no matter how benevolent his ultimate goal of "killing fellows like Mangan" may be, Shotover is bent on finding more and more sophisticated instruments of destruction. Only in the broader perspective supplied by that part of Hector's response to the drumming in the sky at the beginning of act 3 which refers to the possibility that "out of that darkness some new creation will come to supplant us" (159) can we glimpse some conceivably creative outcome of the destructive energies evoked in the play. Out of the destruction of Heartbreak House might arise some new creation of the Life Force. The fires that come from the darkness might burn another Troy and lead to the creation of a new race.

Shaw's lighting specifications in *Heartbreak House* have a clear bearing on the work's metaphorical dimensions and on the complex games it plays with ideas of darkness and light. Although its action is decidedly irregular, the play observes the so-called classical unities of time and place: the action is more or less synchronous with the playing time, and the place remains the same except for the act 3 shift into the garden. In terms of lighting we move from the brightness of the fine, end-of-September evening that can be seen through the window at the beginning of act 1 to the moonless darkness of act 3. In the course of act 1 two lighting changes are introduced. The first is when Hesione goes out into the garden after her exchange with Shotover about his sticks of dynamite. Here the stage direction tells us, *"the evening light is now very red"* (99). Coupled with the dialogue references to Shotover's dynamite, the lighting here conveys a strong hint of the possibility of destructive conflagration and points forward to the fire imagery of the last scene. Toward the end of act 1 the evening light has gone, and the stage is in darkness as Shotover, Hesione, and Hector bewail the folly and futility of Heartbreak House. It has become, literally and metaphorically, a house of darkness.

The darkness onstage is deployed as metaphor in the closing dialogue of act 1. The audience has by this time heard the Shotover rhetoric against Mangan and his world of money-making and greed amplified to its highest pitch in the play. Mangan and his like are "hogs to whom the universe is nothing but a machine for greasing their bristles and filling their snouts" (100). Power of life and death must be gained over these people if the enlightened are to survive. The threats to Heartbreak House come from both within and without. Shotover supplies one image of the latter threat in a curious reference to the forces Mangan and his kind have at their command to unleash: "There are millions of blacks over the water for them to train and let loose on us" (101). In the scene with Hector in which Shotover makes these pronouncements, he sits at his drawing board and *begins to mix a wash of colour*" (101). Shaw creates a paradoxical image here of artistic creation being enlisted in a necessary process of destruction—an image that, it could be argued, obliquely reflects his own project in the creation of *Heartbreak House*, or "The Studio in the Clouds" as the play was once provisionally titled.

The scene with Hector provides an underpinning for the mordant satire of the closing moments of act 1, in which the whole activity of money-making is condemned as belonging to the dark. As Shotover sits down at his table again to continue plying his sinister trade as an inventor of weapons, he replies to Hector's question as to whether he needs more light in which to work, "No. Give me deeper darkness. Money is not made in the light" (105).

Appropriately enough, the next occasion on which the stage is plunged into darkness is when the chief scapegoat of the play's critique of money and greed, Mangan, is left alone after having been hypnotized by Ellie after their scene together at the beginning of act 2. It is as though Ellie, as she steals away and turns the lights out, is leaving Mangan in what many passages of dialogue suggest is his natural element.

At the first sound of the bombing in act 3 ("*a dull distant explosion is heard*" [177]) the Captain blows a warning blast on his whistle and the light on stage again goes out. A naturalistic explanation of this is provided: the police have telephoned with an order to extinguish all lighting. But in context, especially remembering Hector's previous speech about the forces of cosmic change that might emerge "out of that darkness," the extinction of light here has obvious symbolic significance. For a brief instant the play holds out the prospect that an apocalyptic moment has indeed arrived—an idea underlined by Captain Shotover's subsequent command, "Stand by, all hands, for judgement" (178).

Hector's frenzied and reckless behavior in turning on all the lights in the house adds a further dimension to the symbolic pattern Shaw creates here. Mangan and the Burglar run for shelter in the gravel pit, where they are shortly to meet their doom. But those remaining onstage—particularly the trio of Hector, Hesione, and Ellie—confront the possibility of apocalypse with ecstatic desire. Whatever horror and catastrophe the darkness may hold, their stance is one of welcome.

This response is open to several different interpretations. On the one hand, it reflects satirically on the state of the society depicted in the play, implying as it does that anything would be better than the sterile and destructive games played out in Heartbreak House and the multifaceted malaise of its surrounding society. In such a reading the play could be said to end with a form of aborted catharsis. The purging, cleansing fire and annihilation of Heartbreak House invoked as possible conclusions to the action do not come about. The sound of the bombers recedes, and we are left with the comical and richly ironic rendition on Randall's flute of the old World War I patriotic song, "Keep the Home Fires Burning."

On the other hand, it is possible to see this welcome to apocalypse in a different light. Running for safety to the gravel pit or heading for shore like the Church (to recall Captain Shotover's acerbic jest when he hears that the vicarage has been destroyed) are not successful strategies for dealing with danger and the forces of darkness. Perhaps Shaw had in mind, in composing the end of *Heartbreak House*, a passage of dialogue near the end of *Major Barbara*, after the enlightened idealists, Cusins and Barbara, have decided to join forces with the powerful and sinister manufacturer of weapons of destruction, Undershaft:

CUSINS: So the way of life lies through the factory of death?

BARBARA: Yes, through the raising of hell to heaven and of man to God, through the unveiling of an eternal light in the Valley of the Shadow. (3:184)

In the composition of *Heartbreak House* Shaw clearly attached great importance to the contrast between the fair hair of Ellie Dunn and the *"magnificent black hair"* of Hesione (69). The director of the 1920 New York world premiere of *Heartbreak House*, Lawrence Langner, recalls Shaw's displeased response when he was shown a photograph of Effie Shannon in the role of Hesione in this production: "the sharp blue eyes regarded me angrily. 'But she has blond hair—you must have cut one of the lines!'" It is very difficult to believe Langner's further account of this crisis in his early dealings with Shaw. Langner claims that when he explained to Shaw that the line was not cut but "just mumbled," Shaw smilingly said, "That's all right." Shaw was not a dramatist who would have been happy about any of his lines being "just mumbled." Ellie refers to Hesione's "beautiful black hair" not once but twice (125, 166), and on neither occasion could the lines be mumbled. Indeed, the first reference to the hair is associated with a dramatic crisis in Ellie's friendship with Hesione. The possible false-ness of Hesione's hair ("perhaps it comes off at night") represents a further threatened shattering of illusions for Ellie after her discovery about Hector: "(*so taken aback that she drops off the table and runs to her*) Oh, you dont mean to say, Hesione, that your beautiful black hair is false?" (125).

Whatever was done in the New York premiere, there is no question that the dark appearance of Hesione is an integral part of Shaw's conception of her character. In the first stage-direction description of her Shaw directs not only that she should have black hair but that she also be dressed voluptuously *"in a rich robe of black pile"* (70). The costume adds its effect to Ellie's remark when she embraces this dark femme fatale later in act 1, "Hesione: you are a witch" (83).

The contrast between Hesione's and Ellie's appearance plays its part in the subtle, complex development of their relationship and individual characterization during the course of the action. In their first scene together, conventional associations of fair and dark are clearly in operation. The fair young Ellie plays out the role of innocent, naive romantic before the knowing, experienced and mischievous older woman. As the tougher, disillusioned self of Ellie develops, however, the distinction between her and Hesione becomes less clear. In the act 2 scene in which the contrast between their hair color is most clearly foregrounded, Hesione, in a moment of schoolgirlish triumph over her young friend, gives her the mocking nickname of "Goldylocks" [*sic*]

(126). The name was well chosen by Shaw, as Ellie's behavior in the play exactly evokes the ambivalence of her folk-tale counterpart.

As the research of Iona and Peter Opie has shown, the central character in the story of "Goldilocks and the Three Bears" underwent several metamorphoses before she became the golden-haired young maiden named Goldilocks.⁴ In earlier versions of the tale she was a thieving fox named Scrapefoot and an ill-tempered old crone. Her character as a young girl is a mid-Victorian invention, and her present name was not bestowed on her until 1904. The tale contains the ambiguity of its history. In one view Goldilocks is an innocent little potential victim of the angry bears; in another she is an invasive and predatory creature who intrudes herself into other people's houses and helps herself to their belongings.⁵ (Shaw may well have seen a connection with Erica Cotterill and her behavior in his house at Ayot St. Lawrence.)

There are several echoes of the Goldilocks persona in Ellie's portrayal in the play. She falls asleep in someone else's house, which she has entered without being received by hosts. She pours out her tea *"greedily"* (67). Having failed to help herself to somebody else's husband, she helps herself to the Father Bear, "Daddiest" Shotover. Shaw seems to have been keenly aware of the descents into childish greed and predation he provides for his adult personae in the play, and Ellie is a key example of this. Shortly after she has been taunted with the name "Goldylocks" she wails about Hesione's "unfair" share of Hector: "Oh, what right had you to take him all for yourself! (*pulling herself together*) There! You couldn't help it: neither of us could help it" (126).

The embrace between Hesione and Ellie in act 1 anticipates their response to the Beethoven music of the explosions and the sound in the sky in act 3, when they *"throw themselves into one another's arms in wild excitement."* As the company waits *"in silence and intense expectation"* for another bomb after the one that falls in the gravel pit, Hesione and Ellie form a tableau, standing together and tightly holding each other's hands. The fair and dark beauties are bonded in maenadlike joy at the possible release of further destructive energies. The question as to whether they and Hector are to be seen here as possessed by a death-wish or a desire to live life more intensely seems incapable of resolution. Both possibilities are suggested in the dialogue of the last scene. "We of this house are only moths flying into the candle" (180), says Hector to Ellie. But this image closely follows Captain Shotover's declaration, "Courage will not save you; but it will shew that your souls are still alive" (179).

The play leaves us with a choice of possible understandings of the daring/potentially suicidal behavior of Hector, Ellie, and Hesione. But however teasingly ambiguous this behavior may be in intellectual terms, the end of the play is not psychologically unconvincing in the context of the imaginative world Shaw has created in *Heartbreak House*.

7

Preludes of Apocalypse

> Kent. Is this the promis'd end?
> Edgar. Or image of that horror?
>
> *(King Lear, 5.3.262–63)*

"We lived in the atmosphere of the end of civilization."[1] This is how the English poet Stephen Spender described the experience of living during and immediately after World War I—a period that saw the creation of such works as T. S. Eliot's *The Waste Land*, W. B. Yeats's "The Second Coming," D. H. Lawrence's *Women in Love*, and Bernard Shaw's *Heartbreak House*. Yeats's powerful rhetoric in "The Second Coming" of a world being inundated by a "blood-dimmed tide" and given over to "mere anarchy" and Eliot's surreal images in *The Waste Land* of disintegrating cities and "falling towers" were testimony to a time when it must indeed have seemed to many that the end was nigh. Nor is it surprising that this same period awakened in people's minds the ancient myths of the Apocalypse, which incorporate the notion of an ultimate, punitive, and judgmental intervention into human history by the godhead, to the accompaniment of catastrophic physical events such as floods, fires, famine, plague, and other scourges, before the elect are saved and a new divine order established.

The term "apocalypse" derives from the Greek and Latin *apoka-lypsis*, which means "uncovering" or "revelation." Apocalyptic writings purport to be a revelation to the writer of the final outcome of the divine plan of human and celestial history. (In the late twentieth century, under the influence of works of popular culture such as Francis Ford Coppola's film *Apocalypse Now*, the term is tending to undergo a semantic shift and coming to signify the concept of large-scale catastrophes, predictions of which form an essential part of the ancient apocalyptic writings.) Although its roots go back much further in time to Iranian religious systems of the sixth century B.C., Judaic apocalyptic literature flourished most strongly in the period 200 B.C. to A.D. 100. As one commentator puts it, the apocalyptists of this period conceived of themselves as taking part in "the last Act of a stupendous Cosmic Drama begun in the dawn of time" and as belonging to "an age which believed that upon itself had fallen the ends of all the ages, that it was to witness the consummation, the catastrophic curtain to the drama of humanity."[2]

Apocalyptic writing occurs in the Old Testament, as, for example, in the last six chapters of the Book of Daniel (ca. 165 B.C.) and also in the so-called intertestamental literature—a body of Jewish religious writings not included in the biblical canon. The major apocalyptic text of the New Testament is, of course, the Revelation, which is supposed to have been written by Saint John in exile on the island of Patmos near the end of the first century A.D. In the Preface to a religious fable he wrote in 1932, Shaw irreverently described Revelation as "a curious record of the visions of a drug addict" and went on to say that after the promised Second Coming of Christ in A.D. 1000 had failed to eventuate "people were so used to the delay that they readily substituted for the Second Advent a Second Postponement."[3]

What the early Jewish apocalyptic visionaries claim to have had revealed to them is no less than the final working out of God's plan for the universe and His promise for the chosen people of Israel. The apocalyptic writings predict, commonly in esoteric and imaginative symbolism and imagery, an ultimate Judgment Day in which the Godhead enters human history and passes judgment on all humanity. In the divine sphere, this moment is preceded by a decisive war in heaven, in which Satan is overthrown, bound, and cast into the abyss. In the human sphere the day is preceded by a period of immense tribulation, suffering, conflict, and natural disaster of the kind foretold by Jesus in the Gospel According to Matthew: "For nation shall rise against nation, and kingdom against kingdom: and there shall be famines, and pestilences, and earthquakes, in divers places" (24:7). In Revelation seven angels appear with trumpets. As each of the first six of the trumpets sound, the earth is visited with fire and brimstone, seas of blood, earthquakes, plagues, and mass slaughter. At the sound of the seventh trumpet the ultimate transformation of the terrestrial into the celestial is effected, and the perpetual reign of the triumphant Christ over the new Jerusalem commences.

At the moment of apocalypse all opposites are dissolved: the terrestrial becomes the celestial world; the duality of good and evil ends; all time is telescoped in the godhead ("I am Alpha and Omega, the beginning and the end" [Revelation 21:6]); night and day cease to exist. It is this concept of apocalyptic fusion which underlies the famous lines of Wordsworth's *The Prelude*:

> . . . the sick sight
> And giddy prospect of the raving stream,
> The unfettered clouds, and region of the Heavens,
> Tumult and peace, the darkness and the light—
> Were all like workings of one mind, the features
> Of the same face, blossoms upon one tree,
> Characters of the great Apocalypse.[4]

The end of *Heartbreak House* enacts a moment of apocalyptic fusion that similarly brings together an extraordinary range of antithetical experiences and concepts: of horror and joy, destruction and creation, darkness and light, the spheres of heaven and earth. The leap from *Heartbreak House* to other expressions of apocalyptic fusion in English Romantic literature, apart from that just cited in Wordsworth's *The*

Prelude, is not great. Samuel Coleridge's conception of the esemplastic power of the imagination as an echo of the "infinite I AM" in the *Biographia Literaria*, his "ancestral voices prophesying war" in Kubla Khan's "dome of pleasure," and William Blake's marriage of heaven and hell come to mind as notional parallels.[5]

To these examples might be added Milton's expression of the paradoxical mergings that take place in the apocalyptic moment in *Paradise Lost*. Thomas Altizer's description of these mergings suggests interesting conceptual parallels with the end of *Heartbreak House*:

> *Paradise Lost* is the first imaginative vision of the ultimate union of the original act of creation with the movements and acts of fall, atonement, and apocalypse . . . these acts and movements become not only inseparable, but also deeply and comprehensively grounded in the dialectical and paradoxical union of Satan and the Son. This is an apocalyptic union which embodies both a new and radical energy and a new providential order in which good is realized through evil, even if that good is invisible in a now dark-ened cosmos. Yet darkness becomes visible through grace, and then darkness can be manifest as light.[6]

Shaw's stance toward the apocalyptic, however, is essentially playful, ironic, and anticlimactic. In his Apocalypse the trumpets of Revelation are replaced by the comical sound of Randall's flute, and what has actually been effected by the dramatic visitation from heaven, other than the death of Mangan and the Burglar and the destruction of the vicarage, is not revealed. Shaw's play holds out no prophecy— indeed, presents little or no prospect—that good will be "realized through evil," even though "a new and radical energy" might have been sensed in the Beethoven music of the bombers.

Curiously enough, in view of the gulfs between their work in other respects, it is D. H. Lawrence who most closely resembles Shaw in his reactions to the experience of World War I. I am not here con-cerned with questions of influence[7] but rather with what I see as a mutually illuminating comparison between two major works of fiction created at about the same time. Lawrence was writing one of his most overtly apocalyptic novels, *Women in Love*, between April and October

1916, the period that marks the beginning of the composition of *Heartbreak House*. As Frank Kermode pointed out in his seminal essay "Lawrence and the Apocalyptic Types,"[8] the war signaled for Lawrence not simply a time of great crisis in human history but an actual apocalyptic moment. Like Shaw, Lawrence gave a remarkable account of his response to one of the zeppelin raids on England. In a letter to Lady Ottoline Morrell on 9 September 1915, after witnessing a raid on the previous night, he wrote excitedly of a "small golden Zeppelin" sailing above the flashing fires of exploding shells and declared that this was the "war in heaven" of Revelation 7: 7 and of book 6 of Milton's *Paradise Lost*: "It seemed as if the cosmic order were gone, as if there had come a new order . . . it seems our cosmos is burst . . . it is the end—our world is gone, and we are like dust in the air. . . . But there must be a new heaven and a new earth" (Lawrence, 2:390).

In his novel *Kangaroo* Lawrence very precisely fixed the time of the winter of 1915–16 as a period of disintegration of the "old world" and of spiritual collapse. Looking back on this period he described London as a kind of Sodom, in terms that could be taken as a Lawrentian description of Heartbreak House: "the city, in some way, perished . . . from being a heart of the world, and became a vortex of broken passions, lusts, hopes, fears, and horrors."[9] In *D. H. Lawrence: Life into Art* Keith Sagar draws attention to this passage and to Lawrence's sense at this time of a "massive creeping hell"[10] spreading out like a plague over all England and Europe. Lawrence's sense of a creeping, engulfing malaise is strikingly paralleled in one of Shaw's early comments on *Heartbreak House*: "The heartbreak begins, and gets worse until the house breaks out through the windows, and becomes all England with all England's heart broken."[11]

In *Women in Love* the character of Birkin becomes a focal point for agonistic reflection on apocalyptic themes and the whole destiny of the human race. Here again the similarities to some of Shaw's ideas about evolution, which are reflected in *Heartbreak House*, are striking. Hector's speeches about the need for "us useless futile creatures" to be abolished, and the possibility of "some new creation" (159) coming out of the darkness to supplant humanity bear a strong resemblance to several of Birkin's musings in *Women in Love*. The theme to which

Birkin obsessively returns is that man is a failure as an expression of the evolutionary forces of the universe, of the cosmic "creative utterances."[12] For Birkin, "man is a mistake" and "he must go" (*WL*, 142). The coming of the apocalypse, the purging of Sodom, are events to be welcomed rather than feared: "Well, if mankind is destroyed, if our race is destroyed like Sodom, and there is this beautiful evening with the luminous land and trees, I am satisfied. That which informs it all is there, and can never be lost. After all, what is mankind but just one expression of the incomprehensible" (*WL*, 65).

Some of Birkin's musings recall ideas about creative evolution to which Shaw first gave expression in his turn-of-the-century play, *Man and Superman* (composed in 1901–1902), and that were further developed in the work that followed *Heartbreak House*, the five-play cycle *Back to Methuselah*. In Shaw's "religion" of Creative Evolution the human species is seen as simply one of the "innumerable experiments" (2:662)[13] of the Life Force in self-organization, and as a not very successful experiment at that.[14] In "The Revolutionist's Handbook and Pocket Companion" that Shaw appended to *Man and Superman* as purportedly the work of one of the characters in the play, John Tanner, the world is described as a "den of dangerous animals" desperately in need of a new evolutionary development:

> If you know the facts and are strong enough to look them in the face, you must admit that unless we are replaced by a more highly evolved animal—in short, by the Superman—the world must remain a den of dangerous animals among whom our few accidental supermen, our Shakespears, Goethes, Shelleys and their like, must live as precariously as lion tamers do, taking the humor of their situation, and the dignity of their superiority, as a set-off to the horror of the one and the loneliness of the other. (2: 772–73)

In many ways, of course, the worldviews of Lawrence and Shaw are poles apart, but there are also some surprising meeting grounds between these two outsider figures in the early modern period.

One of Lawrence's several Heartbreak Houses in *Women in Love* is Breadalby, the country house presided over by the musically named

Hermione, where unconventional, free-thinking upper-class people gather for house parties and engage in what Birkin/Lawrence see as destructive cerebral conversation. Like Shaw in *Heartbreak House*, Lawrence constructs a powerful female (as well as male) demonology in his novel. Hermione is portrayed as being, for all her interest in culture and refinement, a woman of murderously destructive impulses. Gudrun is even more closely reminiscent of the women of Shaw's *Heartbreak House*. She is sexually magnetic, deploys "vindictive mockery" in the duel of sex, and reduces her lover/enemy, Gerald, to the state of an "infant . . . Don Juan" whom she would cheerfully murder, and in fact does destroy (*WL*, 272, 254).[15] In both play and novel the demonic female is seen as a central part of a Sodomitic culture of "Dead Sea Fruit" (*WL*, 140) that is ripe for its apocalyptic moment of purgation.

The introduction of apocalyptic themes into fictional structures—the primary affiliations of which are with naturalism—posed certain artistic problems that Shaw and Lawrence handled in different ways. In Lawrence's novel it is Ursula who puts the idea of apocalypse into perspective as a "fantasy." Ursula is attracted by Birkin's "pleasant fancy" about the desirability of abolishing humanity but is all too aware of the "hideous actuality" of humanity: she knows "it could not disappear so cleanly and conveniently" (*WL*, 142). In *Heartbreak House* the prospect of apocalypse held out in the speeches of Hector and Shotover in act 3 is not fulfilled.[16] The play ends in anticlimax. There is no revelation, and there is only a partial judgment, in the form of the death of Mangan and Billy Dunn. Shaw's remarks in the Preface to *Heartbreak House* about people's disappointed expectations that "the shock of the war would automatically make a new heaven and a new earth" (55) suggest an analogy in real life to the anticlimactic close of his comedy.

What *Heartbreak House* presents us with is not an apocalyptic moment but an exploration of the games being played out as society drifts toward the abyss. It is a play about the preludes of apocalypse. The ancient myth is employed as a rhetorical tool in a powerful critique of contemporary society. The behavior of the characters in

Heartbreak House is reminiscent of the biblical accounts of the careless mortals in the days before the flood:

> For as in the days that were before the flood they were eating and drinking, marrying and giving in marriage, until the day that Noe entered into the ark,
> And knew not until the flood came, and took them all away.[17]

Part of the force of the end of Shaw's play, however, lies in the fact that the "flood" does not arrive. There is no new heaven and no new earth, and, instead of Revelation, we are left with an amateurish rendition of the tune of a sentimental war song and the sardonic reflection that Heartbreak House still stands.

In the Preface to *Heartbreak House* Shaw writes of "the terrible castigation of comedy, the ruthless light of laughter that glares on the stage" (57). In the longer view, the sentimental patriotism enshrined in such popular songs as "Keep the Home Fires Burning" (which in the midst of conflict make extraordinarily powerful contributions to the maintenance of national morale and solidarity) can seem either absurd or grotesque. But Shaw's remarks about comedy serve not only to remind us of his own firm sense of the genre to which his play belongs but also to underline its satirical character. I have already drawn attention to autobiographical dimensions of *Heartbreak House* that have been underestimated and insufficiently explored as shaping influences in its composition. But the play also, of course, inhabits the public domain of satire. It creates a complex image of a whole society in dangerous disarray, and presents, in imaginative terms, a fierce "castigation" of its folly and evil.

By the time *Heartbreak House* came to be published in 1919, Shaw had produced, in the play itself and its Preface, what are in effect two parallel critiques of contemporary society. There is clearly substantial thematic continuity between play and Preface, but they are not saying the same things in different ways. The Preface is at once more specific and more abstract than the play. It historicizes Heartbreak House firmly as "cultured, leisured Europe before the war," and (as does not occur in the play) there are several references to the war as a quasi-apocalyptic event:

> For four years she [Nature] smote our firstborn and heaped on us plagues of which Egypt never dreamed. (18)
>> Thus were the firstborn of Heartbreak House smitten. (22)
>> England, inviolate for so many centuries that the swoop of war on her homesteads had long since ceased to be more credible than a return of the Flood, could hardly be expected to keep her temper sweet. (26)

The Preface also supplies a larger perspective on the historical and intellectual processes that gave rise to the catastrophe of the war and the predicament of *Heartbreak House*. Part of Shaw's argument in the Preface is that the war was a long-delayed retribution (by "Nature" in this secularized version of apocalypse) for a combination of "indifference" and "false doctrine" in what he calls "The Wicked Half Century," the second half of the nineteenth (18). Like his mentor, Samuel Butler, Shaw believed that Darwinism had fostered a ruthless new "religion" in which ethics, human purpose and moral choice were marginalized, or exiled, in favor of a type of secular Calvinism that deemed that human destiny was not capable of being influenced by the exercise of the human will. Darwin's theories, along with other developments in the natural sciences, had seemed to validate attitudes of aggressive and predatory competition, and to elevate the struggle for survival to the plane of a religion. The catastrophe of the war is seen by Shaw as one of the major outcomes of this new "religion": "We taught Prussia this religion; and Prussia bettered our instruction so effectively that we presently found ourselves confronted with the necessity of destroying Prussia to prevent Prussia destroying us" (19).

In the play itself there is no specific reference to these ideas about Darwinism and "The Wicked Half Century." But there are other ways in which these underlying preoccupations are reflected in *Heartbreak House*. In the Preface to *Back to Methuselah* Shaw directly links Darwinism with the abuses of profiteering capitalism, in a scathing section of the essay entitled "Why Darwinism Pleased the Profiteers" (5:315–16). This is anticipated in *Heartbreak House* in the various attacks on the "hogs" of business "to whom the universe is nothing but a machine for greasing their bristles and filling their snouts" (100). When Mangan, as "a man that knows how to take care of himself," explains to Ellie his philosophy of business he reveals himself as a cunning, ruthless predator on his fellow creatures: "Business is business; and I ruined him [Mazzini] as a matter of business" (108).

A further image of the capitalist boss as predator is developed in a speech by Hesione to Mazzini regarding the proposed marriage between Mangan and Ellie: "Are you going to fling your delicate, sweet, helpless child into such a beast's claws . . . ?" This question follows Hesione's description of Mangan as a "slavedriver . . . a man accustomed to have great masses of iron beaten into shape for him by steam hammers! to fight with women and girls over a halfpenny an hour ruthlessly! a captain of industry, I think you call him, dont you?" (116). The irony of Hesione's description of Ellie as a "sweet, helpless child" can hardly be lost on an audience that has just seen the same young woman reduce Mangan to impotent rage before sending him off into an hypnotic trance.

We know from some of Shaw's letters written during and after World War I that one of the models for Mangan was Lord Devonport, a prominent businessman and former MP who was elevated to the peerage and served as Food Controller from 1916 to 1917 (*Letters*, 3: 505, 513, 744). Devonport, the head of a large wholesale grocery firm, was one of a number of people from the business world, with obvious vested interests in their posts, whom Lloyd George appointed to his wartime government. Devonport's blunders as Food Controller led to his resignation from the post in May 1917—a fact that possibly underlies the laughter created by Mangan among the other characters when he explains that he was appointed to his position because of his credentials "as a practical business man" (163).[18]

As I have pointed out elsewhere,[19] however, it seems likely that in creating Mangan, Shaw also had in mind the well-known nineteenth-century Irish poet James Clarence Mangan, one of whose best-known poems is "The Nameless One." The subject of this poem is a commonplace man, in "hoary" middle-age, who is condemned to "herd with demons," who is "betray'd in friendship, befool'd in love, /

With spirit shipwreck'd."[20] The dual image of Mangan in the play as predator/victim reflects these two different models of his character. But even though the play is a far more complex text than its Preface, it leaves us in no doubt that rampant, predatory capitalism and social Darwinism are part of the root causes of the condition, ripe for apocalypse, into which civilization has drifted. The problem for the inhabitants of Heartbreak House is that although they can effectively ridicule Mangan, they are powerless to control the forces he represents. Their impotence is compounded by indifference and their self-diversion into futile games of love-making.

The offstage figure of Hastings Utterword presents another dimension of the Darwinian macrocosm in which Heartbreak House is situated. Early in the play Captain Shotover's opinion of Utterword is made clear when he refers to Ariadne as being "in a remote part of the Empire with her numskull of a husband," paying the latter the dubious compliment of resembling his ship's figurehead: "He had the same expression: wooden yet enterprising" (63). In the real world evoked in the play, however, figures such as Hastings Utterword (whose first name is probably intended to recall that of the colonial administrator, Warren Hastings, who rose to prominence in the East India Company and became the first British governor-general of Bengal) wielded immense power in the commercially based enterprises of empire, which constitute a further dimension of the forces of predation and conquest represented by Mangan. When Mangan challenges Lady Utterword with the question, "Who else is there but me?," she replies, "There is Hastings. Get rid of your ridiculous sham democracy; and give Hastings the necessary powers, and a good supply of bamboo to bring the British native to his senses: he will save the country with the greatest ease" (165).

In this passage the conquistador forces of capitalism and imperialism are brought into direct association with each other. As Mangan ruthlessly subordinates men, women, and children in his factories, so Utterword subordinates entire races of people. Shaw's attitude toward imperialism was in fact more complicated than is suggested here. He was consistently critical of imperialistic expansionism and its concomitant exploitation and oppression. As Patricia Pugh points out, in an excellent analysis of Shaw's various pronouncements about imperialism, he was also persuaded of "the inevitable dissolution of empire."[21] But in the manifesto "Fabianism and the Empire," which Shaw drafted in 1900, he argued that because the British empire was a fait accompli at that time, what was needed was not simple opposition to the existence of the empire but the implementation of enlightened and humane administration in place of rapacious self-interest and class conflict. Shaw's ideal outcome for the British empire was the eventual formation of a federation or commonwealth of self-governing, independent nations. Whatever more temperate views Shaw may have espoused about empire in his nondramatic writings, however, its representative in *Heartbreak House*, Hastings Utterword, the subduer of natives with "bamboo," can hardly be taken very seriously as the potential savior of England that Ariadne sees him as being.

In his treatment of capitalism in this play Shaw had come a long way from the spirit of his earlier portrait of an industrial tycoon, the munitions manufacturer Andrew Undershaft in *Major Barbara* (1905). In the earlier play (to the dismay of some of his socialist friends at the time and later critics of both the left and right) Shaw flirted with the idea of a trilateral alliance between the irresistible power represented by Undershaft, the spirituality represented by his salvationist daughter, Major Barbara, and the philosophical intelligence represented by the classics scholar, Cusins. This trinity of forces formed at the end of the play—with Barbara's mother, Lady Britomart, as an influential figure in the background—is to rule over the future fortunes of Undershaft's empire and his model town of Perivale St. Andrews.

While Undershaft is a ruthless and utterly unscrupulous operator as an international seller of arms to anyone prepared to pay, and whose Darwinian motto is "Thou shalt starve ere I starve" (*MB*, 173), as a boss he is quite different from Boss Mangan. He provides superb working conditions, facilities, and accommodation for his work force—a far cry from the wretched squalor Barbara tries to ameliorate in her West Ham Salvation Army shelter—and he is affectionately known among the employees as "Dandy Andy" (*MB*, 158). Shaw was aware of the strains his fantasy of such an alliance as that proposed between Undershaft, Barbara, and Cusins creates in the last act of

Major Barbara. Nevertheless, his Undershaft is a powerful and challenging creation, and the portrait of the potentially benign face of capitalism in Perivale St. Andrews is a long way from socialist orthodoxies. In keeping with the trade invented for him, Undershaft became a loose cannon in the Shavian intellectual universe, or, to change metaphor, an attractive monster his creator was not quite able to control.

In some ways *Heartbreak House* can be seen as Shaw's "answer" to this earlier work: *Major Barbara* is another text with which *Heartbreak House* critically interacts. The portrayal of Mangan contains some echoes of that of Undershaft. He is presented as a powerful, ruthless survivor in a dog-eat-dog world of business. Like Undershaft, too, his power sets him above the ordinary processes of democratic government. "Government of your country! *I* am the Government of your country" (*MB*, 151), declares Undershaft to his son Stephen. "The Prime Minister of this country asked me to join the Government without even going through the nonsense of an election, as the dictator of a great public department" (163), Mangan tells the assembled company in act 3 of *Heartbreak House.*

Mangan, however, entirely lacks the charisma, wit, and capacity to charm of Undershaft. In some respects Mangan harks back to the contemptible capitalists of Shaw's earliest plays—the rackrenting landlord and grinder of the face of the poor, Sartorius, in *Widower's Houses,* and the obnoxious Sir George Crofts in *Mrs. Warren's Profession.* The audience of *Heartbreak House* is even left in some doubt as to the existence of Mangan's central power base—his money. Like Lewis Carrol's Cheshire Cat, it is sometimes there and sometimes not. When Mangan startles the company and pulls the mat from beneath a major premise of the action of the play by declaring that he has "no money" (162), he recalls the fraudulent financier Merdle in Dickens's *Little Dorritt,* whose financial empire is discovered, following his suicide in a bath, to be entirely bogus and worthless.

The idea suggested in Barbara's alliance with her father at the end of *Major Barbara*—that wealth might be invested with some redeeming spiritual influence or might create environments in which spiritual values can be realized—is in *Heartbreak House* raised only to be eventually put down. In the earlier play Undershaft is armed with the argument that values such as honor, justice, love, and mercy can only be realized in circumstances of material well-being and security. Such values are "the graces and luxuries of a rich, strong, and safe life" (*MB*, 116). Poverty is a crime committed by society at large because it creates the circumstances in which the worst aspects of human conduct are encouraged and militates against the expression of the nobler side of human nature. There is a clear echo of Undershaft's philosophy in *Heartbreak House* when Ellie Dunn instructs Shotover in her new-fashioned understanding of the relation between souls and money: "ELLIE. . . . Old-fashioned people think you can have a soul without money. They think the less money you have, the more soul you have. Young people nowadays know better. A soul is a very expensive thing to keep: much more so than a motor car" (143).

Ellie's intention in pretending to sell herself to Mangan is to save her soul from "the poverty that is damning [her] by inches" (145). But a crucial difference between *Heartbreak House* and *Major Barbara* in this area of thematic concern is that Ellie moves beyond this state of understanding and repudiates her own argument in this act 2 scene with Captain Shotover. At the moment she discovers that her real goal is "life with a blessing," she also discovers the real reason she could not

Albert Perry as Captain Shotover and Elizabeth Risdon as Ellie Dunn in a scene from act 2 of *Heartbreak House*, Garrick Theater, New York, 1920; set design by Lee Simonson. *Photograph by Francis Bruguiere. Used by permission of the British Library.*

marry Mangan. She names several things on which there is a blessing but says that "on Mr Mangan's money there is none" (169).

Significantly, in *Heartbreak House* it is the arch enemy of capitalism, Captain Shotover, who is identified with the creation of munitions. As an inventor of weapons of destruction, it is he who is trying, with paranoic hostility, to wrest the power over life and death from the likes of Mangan and the "Foreign Office toff" and idle amorist, Randall:

HECTOR. Are Mangan's bristles worse than Randall's lovelocks?

SHOTOVER. We must win powers of life and death over them both. I refuse to die until I have invented the means. (90, 100)

Shotover's speech here can be read as a cancellation of the Fabian notions that seem to underlie the conclusion of *Major Barbara*, of infiltrating the centers of capitalist power and converting them to more enlightened and spiritually informed states.

Central to Shaw's argument in the Preface to *Heartbreak House* is the idea, also present in the play, that power and culture had become dangerously dissociated from each other. They were in "separate compartments" (15). The cultivated voluptuaries in the Heartbreak House that, as Shaw argued in the Preface, the whole of "cultured, leisured Europe" had become in the period of human history leading up to World War I, had failed to engage with the realities of power in society and had retreated into a Capua of self-indulgence in refined literary and artistic pleasures—romance and love-making. In the meantime, power was being wielded by people of far less intelligence and sensibility, the numskulls of politics and empire and the hogs of big business. Love, in this Europe-wide Heartbreak House Shaw sketches in the Preface, was elevated to the status of a supreme value but was in fact a veneer, covering up more sinister convictions: "Heartbreak House . . . rhapsodized about love; but it believed in cruelty" (22).

In *Heartbreak House* Shaw presents a view of relations between the sexes as permeated with the same forces of social Darwinism as those that operate in the domains of politics and business. Cruelty, and subordination of the other, are two of the reigning principles in the conduct of sexual relations throughout the play's action.

Randall's complaint to Hector that "some of your games in this house are damned annoying, let me tell you" (151) occurs in a discussion between the two that simultaneously brings into focus the major theme of game-playing in *Heartbreak House* and the metatheatrical character of the work. The dialogue in which this speech of Randall's is situated is about "posing." Hector has been saying that jealousy does not fit well with Randall's "easy man-of-the-world pose" (151). Hector's next speech telescopes the notions of game-playing, posing, and dramatic roles in such a way as to remove the space between theatrical and "real" worlds. In a speech that supplies a sharp focus on Shaw's sense of the ludic properties of his play and of the construction of human character and identity in general, Hector maintains that being a gentleman "is a pose like any other": "In this house we know all the poses: our game is to find out the man under the pose. The man under your pose is apparently Ellie's favourite, Othello" (151). In other words, the inner man, the "real person" beneath the surface of Randall's poses, is suggested here to be a fictional creation in another play. Thus the implied conception of identity here involves a form of circularity, or infinite regression into fiction, not unlike that deployed in Luigi Pirandello's *Six Characters in Search of an Author*.

The comedy of this act 2 exchange between Hector and Randall is enriched by the fact that of all the play's characters Hector obviously takes the prize as the chief poseur in *Heartbreak House*. At his first introduction in the play we learn that he has been posing as the romantic Marcus Darnley and enchanting Ellie with his Othello-like tales of adventure. Before act 1 is complete the audience witnesses Hector, left alone onstage, fighting an imaginary duel with his walking stick as a weapon and then seizing an imaginary woman, presumably the one he has fought the imaginary duel for. In the lead-up to the theatrical climax of the Burglar's arrival, Hector enters dressed up like Lawrence of Arabia in "*a handsome Arab costume*" (130).

Hector's act 1 fantasy of dueling and conquest is part of a pervasive evocation of the world of children and of childish games and behavior. His surname, Hushabye, recalls a nursery rhyme that contains in its verses a miniature version of apocalyptic warning and subtly brings together the ideas of the nurserylike behavior and games of the adults in the house and their threatened doom:

> Hushabye baby, on the tree top
> When the wind blows the cradle will rock
> When the bough breaks the cradle will fall
> Down will come baby, cradle and all.

Seemingly in allusion to this nursery rhyme, as the bombs are falling in act 3 Nurse Guinness goes to the hammock in which Ariadne remains reclining and waits there *"as if it were by Ariadne's cradle"* (178). The fact that the household affairs of Heartbreak House are still presided over by the Nurse is one of several other ways in which the nursery world is evoked. When Ariadne returns home she reacts violently to the idea of sleeping in her old room and objects to Nurse Guinness addressing her as "Miss" and "lovey" (65). At the same time, however, she is shown as wanting to recover Shotover's paternal affection for her as a child and unavailingly introduces herself to him by her childhood name of "little Paddy Patkins" (156). Later, a vivid image of Ariadne's nursery self is supplied in Hector's question to Randall about his folly in allowing Ariadne to drag him about and beat him "as a toy donkey is dragged about and beaten by a child" (156).

Shaw also endows Hesione and Ellie ("Miss Hessy" and "ducky" as they are respectively dubbed early in the play by Nurse Guinness [62]) with mischievous, little-girl selves, as we have seen in such instances as the Goldilocks scene, the teasing and bullying of Mangan, and Ellie's childish protests about Hesione's stealing of her "babies" (126). Apart from Ellie, all of the characters are either old or middle-aged. But Shaw continually creates images of the behavior of the inhabitants of Heartbreak House as being like that of grown-up children in a shiplike setting that itself evokes the fantasies of childhood play.[22]

As well as creating characters whose game-playing of various kinds represents a major part of their fictional identity, Shaw also reveals a sharp consciousness of his own game-playing in the composition of the play. From early in act 1 the atmosphere is charged with interspersed metatheatrical and metafictional jokes. Ariadne, within a few minutes of her arrival, is accused by Shotover of "impersonating" herself. Hector later tells her, "You are not to be trusted. You have made a scene"—a motif picked up in his subsequent conversation with Randall when he says that Ariadne "does nothing but make scenes from morning till night" (141, 151). Hesione's act 1 question to Ellie, as she spots the volume of Shakespeare she has been reading, "Quite sure youre not in love with an actor?" (78), precipitates a veritable Chinese puzzle of interconnected fictions, involving Ellie's fantasies of a "white" Othello and of her Marcus Darnley, the character in Shakespeare's play, and the fertile breed of Hector's "made-up stories" and false tigers (78–79, 85).

The highly self-conscious character of the play becomes even more pronounced as the action moves through the theatrical climax of the Burglar scene in act 2 to the sensational but anticlimactic close of act 3. The introduction of the Burglar brings on some outrageous uses of coincidence and constitutes a fine example of the Dickensian "mixture of popular and serious art" in Shaw's work that the English novelist Angus Wilson found so engaging and significant.[23] Not only does the Burglar turn out to be Shotover's disreputable and untrustworthy former boatswain, but it is also revealed that he is the former husband of Nurse Guinness—an undesirable connection she has apparently kept secret from the Shotover family for several decades. After the Burglar has been ordered off by Shotover, the playful conversation between author and audience can again be heard in Hesione's summary of the Burglar episode: "Well, we have had a very exciting evening. Everything will be an anticlimax after it" (139).

In act 3, as the agony of inactivity and misery onstage reaches a peak in the tearful departure of Mangan for a walk in the dark with Hesione, Hector must surely voice the thoughts of most audiences of the play when he impatiently asks, "How is all this going to end?" (174). A final flourishing of metatheatrical cap and bells comes in the last two lines of dialogue, which can be interpreted as simultaneously referring to the receding invaders from Hector's metaphysical darkness and the return of another audience at the next night's performance of the play, at the end of which the magnificent drumming in the sky (for the representation of which Shaw suggested a powerful vacuum cleaner) will of course return, and again recede:

MRS HUSHABYE. . . . What a glorious experience! I hope theyll come again tomorrow night.

ELLIE. . . . Oh, I hope so.

The political environment of early apocalyptic literature was one of conquest and oppression. In A.D. 70, Around the time the book of Revelation is thought to have been written, a climactic moment of Armageddon-like dimensions was reached in the pattern of domination by external powers that for centuries had characterized the history of Jerusalem and the Israelites. Shortly before the Passover, when the city was overcrowded with people and famine and plague were rife, the Holy City was invaded by a large force of Roman soldiers, who had been ordered by the Emperor Vespasian to put down widespread rebellion against Roman rule. The city was razed, more than a million of its inhabitants were slaughtered, and the Temple, the central place of Jewish worship, was destroyed by fire.

As one recent commentator on apocalyptic structures in contemporary U.S. and Latin American fiction put it, both the early Hebrew and early Christian apocalyptic texts describe the end of the world "from the point of view of a narrator who is radically opposed to existing spiritual and political practices . . . his narrative reflects not only his opposition to existing practices but also his political powerlessness to change them. His is a subversive vision."[24] This accurately describes the situation of such writers as Shaw and Lawrence, who turned to apocalyptic literary forms in the middle years of World War I. Shaw had been reviled and ostracized for his acerbic pamphlet, "Common Sense about the War" (which of course did nothing to alter the course of political events). Lawrence and his German wife, Frieda, were hounded by British police as suspected enemy agents in the farmhouse to which they had retreated at Zennor in Cornwall and were subjected to extraordinary pressures of social alienation. Both Shaw and Lawrence engaged themselves in wars of words against and denunciations of the social and political cultures of their time.

The biblical apocalyptists were engaged in a twofold project. On the one hand, their writings were intended as an exhortation to maintain the faith that, at an appointed time, the present tribulations would be brought to an end by divine intervention, that the opponents and oppressors of God's chosen people would be punished and vanquished, and that a new heaven and earth would be established. On the other hand, the writers of the apocalyptic texts were also engaged in ferocious castigation of the immoral behavior, abominations, and idolatrous practices of those to whom their writings were addressed. In *Heartbreak House* Shaw positions himself in relation to the apocalyptic tradition as both an imitator and skeptical parodist. He adopts the apocalyptic writer's role—that of scathing critic and portender of doom. Still, he could hardly have his play express the naive prediction that "out of that darkness" to which Hector alludes would come the new Jerusalem.

In a letter written shortly after the completion of the play, Shaw specifically compares Captain Shotover to Jeremiah, one of the most strident of the Old Testament denouncers of the wickedness of his times. As this letter continues it recalls a constantly recurrent theme in the apocalyptic writings—that of the sexual aberrations of the people. But, more importantly, the letter also indicates Shaw's sense at the time that the perplexing quality of the play derives from the fact that it contains promises that fizzle out:

> The old Captain is your prophet Jeremiah bawling the judgement of God on all this insanity. And you have the undercurrent of sex continually reproducing quicksand as fast as the welter tries to consolidate itself. . . . I think what makes [the play] puzzling is that the people seem to be so interesting and attractive at first sight that one is led to expect great things from them; and when they are all reduced to absurdity, and even the solution of blowing them to bits misses fire, the spectator feels baffled and disappointed, as if something very promising had been wantonly spoilt. (*Letters*, 3:513)

The dialogue that Shaw creates with the apocalyptic tradition in *Heartbreak House*, at once imitative and parodic, recalls the play's other intertextual relations.

The sacred revelations of the apocalyptic tradition are displaced in Shaw's play by revelations that are all theatrical and mostly farcical in character. "Marcus Darnley" is revealed to be Hector Hushabye and the husband of his female admirer's friend. The Burglar is revealed to be not only the former boatswain of Captain Shotover but also the former husband of Nurse Guinness. It is revealed that Mangan has "no money." Ellie Dunn suddenly reveals in act 3 that the whole question of her marriage prospects has been resolved by the acquisition of her "spiritual husband," Captain Shotover.

Hesione's remark that "everything will be an anti-climax" after the "very exciting evening" (139) that has climaxed in the arrival and apprehension of the Burglar takes on a special significance in the context of a work that taps into the apocalyptic tradition. The ancient apocalyptic writings predict a climax to end all climaxes, the final working out of a "sacred masterplot" (Zamora, 45) that will bring to an end the whole "story" of humanity and the cosmos. But all apocalyptic writing involves tension between the notion of ultimate narrative closure and the awareness of continuing history. In later, secular apocalyptic literature the orderly narrative of apocalypse comes into tension not only with the disorderly, open-ended narrative of history but also with the consciousness that "the promis'd end" is notorious for not eventuating. With the climax of the Burglar episode, Shaw creates a farcical rival to the various unfulfilled hints of apocalyptic climax in act 3.

The Burglar episode does have its critics, and in Anthony Page's 1983 production of the play the scene was cut altogether.[25] But the scene is both thematically and structurally important. The Burglar cements the association created in the play between capitalist enterprise, the possession of property (such as Ariadne's diamonds), and theft. (Shaw was fond of quoting Proudhon's saying that "property is theft.")[26] The Burglar is an unlicensed member of a society of thieves. Despite the apparently random, fantasialike character of the construction of *Heartbreak House*, the Burglar episode has been well prepared

Henry Travers as The Burglar (Billy Dunn) in *Heartbreak House*, Garrick Theater, New York, 1920. *Photograph by Ira D. Schwarz. Used by permission of the British Library.*

for in numerous earlier references to the scoundrel Billy Dunn. In this sense the Burglar has become an old friend, as it were, of the audience by the time he arrives. Structurally the scene serves to underline the absence of a truly apocalyptic and transforming moment at the play's end. In the Gospel of Matthew and in Revelation the thief who visits the unwary in the night is a typological figure of the Second Coming of Christ:

> But know this, that if the goodman of the house had known in what watch the thief would come, he would have watched, and would not have suffered his house to be broken up.
>
> Therefore be ye also ready: for in such an hour as ye think not the Son of man cometh. (Matthew 24:43–44)
>
> I have not found thy works perfect before God. . . . If therefore thou shalt not watch, I will come on thee as a thief, and thou shalt not know what hour I will come upon thee. (Revelation 3:2–3)

Shaw's introduction of the self-righteous and sanctimonious Burglar, who visits the unwary house of "goodman" Shotover in the night, creates wildly comic echoes of these biblical passages.

Heartbreak House concludes with a comical last trump[27] in the form of a musical quotation from a popular song of the time in which the play was written, Ivor Novello's "Keep the Home Fires Burning (Till the Boys Come Home)," with words by Lena Guilbert Ford, which was composed at the end of 1914 and achieved instant popularity.[28] The song encapsulated the spirit of fervent patriotism and sentimental dedication to the cause, which attended Britain's entry into World War I. The "stirring call" had been answered, and "the boys" had been summoned from "the hillside" and "the glen" (and, incidentally, from the *ultima thules* of empire)[29] to "help a nation [Belgium] in distress." The song, itself a quaint simulacrum of an apocalyptic text, refers to a present period of heartbreak but also to a silver lining in the dark cloud and the need to "turn the dark cloud inside out":

> . . . although your heart is break-ing,
> Make it sing this chee-ry song.

Keep the home fires burn-ing,
While your hearts are year-ning,
Though your lads are far a-way
They dream of Home;
There's a sil-ver lin-ing
Through the dark cloud shi-ning
Turn the dark cloud in-side out,
Till the boys come Home.

Shaw's invocation of this song at the end of *Heartbreak House* creates a complex dramatic moment. Randall's success in getting out the simple tune of "Keep the Home Fires Burning" on his flute returns the play from the Beethoven music of the bombers to the sphere of farcical comedy. For almost the entire length of act 3 Randall has been confined to his room like a naughty child. His only communication with the others has been a rebellious reply on his flute when Ariadne reprimands him for not having gone to bed. When the bombing begins Randall rushes onstage in his pajamas, *"distractedly waving a flute,"* and tries to persuade Ariadne to take refuge in the cellar. Her response is to issue instructions to Randall to show he is not afraid, to "be good" and to play "Keep the Home Fires Burning" (179). His playing at the end is thus his final act of subservience to this stern mistress.

In context, the words of the song contain more than one sardonic double entendre. When Ariadne names the song, Nurse Guinness remarks, "*(grimly)* Theyll keep the home fires burning for us: them up there" (179). By the time *Heartbreak House* was being written destruction of civilian dwellings by fire, as the result of bombing raids, had become commonplace in the towns and cities of southern England. As tens of thousands of "the boys" did not "come home" during the terrible years of 1915–18, the song itself must have acquired extraordinary dimensions of sadness. A further twist to the song title in Shaw's play is added when Ellie implores "Marcus"/Hector to "set fire to the house" (179). The patriotic song is here involved in an ironic comment on the capacity, and even desire, of Heartbreak House to self-destruct.

The sentiments of Ivor Novello's song would have been repugnant to Shaw. While not a pacifist, he condemned the whole syndrome of sentimental patriotism and propaganda in which Britain was caught up at the beginning of World War I. In a playlet he wrote in 1915, *O'Flaherty V.C.*, Shaw has his hero, the philosophical Private O'Flaherty, conclude, "Youll never have a quiet world til you knock the patriotism out of the human race" (4:1000). In "Common Sense about the War" he attacked the main pretext of Britain's entry into the war—the preservation of Belgian neutrality (alluded to in Novello's song as "the sacred call of friend"—as a sham.

Shaw was especially appalled by the way in which the women of England, with whom the home-keeping themes of Novello's song must have been powerfully associated, became caught up in the war fever, and he stunned an audience in London in 1915 by comparing women of the day in Britain to the Bacchantes in Euripides' *The Bacchae*. In this play Agave, the mother of King Pentheus, joins the frenzied worshipers of Dionysus in a destructive orgy in which they seek to tear the wild beasts of the mountains limb from limb. In the morning Agave finds that she is holding in her hands not the head of a wild beast she thought she had severed but that of her own son, King Pentheus. Having recalled this tragic story in a speech at King's Hall, Covent Garden, on 26 October 1915, Shaw went on to say that "there are women in Britain today who have gone mad in the pursuit of the wild beasts, who are killing Germans with their mouths. On the morrow when they awake after their frenzy they will find in their laps the heads of their slaughtered sons."[30] The bold, almost bathetic, dramatic device of using Randall's successful performance of the tune of "Keep the Home Fires Burning" as the closing moment of *Heartbreak House* carries with it a powerful set of satirical messages. After the fleeting prospects of apocalypse and "Judgment" held out in act 3, the World War I song recalls us to the chaos and folly of history.[31]

Conclusion

In this study I have explored *Heartbreak House* in its historical, biographical, theatrical, and literary contexts. The play is complex and Janus-faced. In some ways it presents itself as a work about large public issues, looking critically and satirically at a society that is seen to be in dangerous disarray and on the brink of destruction. But the play also reflects, in a number of subtle and disguised ways, some of Shaw's own comic and painful experiences in the period leading up to World War I. In the Preface Shaw emphasizes the intellectual and social origins of the malaise that resulted in the catastrophe of World War I. He characterizes the second half of the nineteenth century as "The Wicked Half Century" in which Darwinism and scientific materialism encouraged the "banishment of conscience from human affairs" (18, 20). Such themes are certainly reflected in the play, but the play and Preface should be seen not as texts saying the same things in different ways but as parallel critiques of the society Heartbreak House symbolizes. The play is much less historically specific than the Preface; very much to the foreground in the play, as distinct from the Preface, are the cruel, manipulative, and often childish games pursued in the duel of sex. The Preface provides no hint of the play's autobiographical dimensions that I have examined here.

In writing *Heartbreak House* Shaw continually conducts witty and parodic dialogues with other texts—works belonging to genres ranging from *The Iliad* to early twentieth-century plays by Anton Chekhov. The numerous echoes of other texts and literary motifs in the play are creatively transformed in Shaw's treatment of them into quite different keys. The many literary burglaries detectable in the play can be seen to have been Shavianized in distinctive and amusing ways. Captain Shotover's shiplike house is related to a tradition of such houses in nineteenth-century fiction, but whereas the latter are all places of orderly snugness, hospitality, human warmth, and security, the Shotover house represents a kind of reversal or travesty of the fictional tradition to which it belongs. It is disorderly and untidy, unwelcoming to guests, and profoundly insecure—a "house without foundations" (171).

Many critics have commented on the numerous echoes of Shakespeare and Chekhov in *Heartbreak House*. In my reexamination of the play's links with Shakespearean and Chekhovian texts here I have shown that, in most cases where Shaw can be seen as an imitator of those dramatists, difference from the original matters as much as similarity. While he is obviously indebted to Shakespearean and Chekhovian texts, his play creates a lively counter-discourse in its relation to them.

In the structure of *Heartbreak House* and in its depiction of character Shaw adopted deliberately disconcerting and destabilizing strategies. The play's form is quite remote from the dramatic model established in the nineteenth century's well-made plays, with their carefully developed, intricate plots and dénouements in which all the threads of narrative are carefully drawn together. In contrast, Shaw's "fantasia" develops as a kaleidoscopic series of encounters, coquetry, sexual passes, stratagems, snatches of philosophy, quarrels, and character assassinations. Most of the narrative motifs generated during the play remain unresolved. As a group the characters are presented in deeply ambiguous lights, at one moment seen as "heartbroken imbeciles" and in the next as "rather a favourable specimen of what is best in . . . English culture" (173). Ambiguity is also a pervasive feature of the portrayal of the individual characters. It is testimony to Shaw's great powers as a dramatist that he was able to control the extraordinarily volatile energies let loose in the play and create a work that has repeatedly proven its theatrical strength over the decades since its first production in 1920.

Heartbreak House is rooted in the tradition of nineteenth-century naturalism. But the play strains at the limits of naturalistic conventions and gains increasingly symbolic dimensions as its scenes unfold. The travelers in Captain Shotover's shiplike house become a society on the edge of doom. The ship is England heading for the rocks, unless it learns navigation, and the sailors are like the unwatchful inhabitants of the earth referred to in the ancient prophecies of apocalypse. Suggestions of demonic and other supernatural forces in the cosmos are scattered throughout in the characterization and dialogue.

The word "prelude" derives from the medieval Latin *praeludium*, which means "preliminary play, before the real performance." (The medieval word is, in turn, derived from the classical Latin verb *praeludere*, "to play beforehand.") The games played by the characters in *Heartbreak House* are revealed, as the play proceeds, as the games of a profoundly unstable and potentially doomed society. The members of this society are seen to be responding to their predicament either by dreaming up horrendous weapons of destruction, like Captain Shotover's, in the hope of gaining control over surrounding forces of alienation, or engaging in futile and destructive games of romance and flirtation or talk. Despite the grimness of these themes, however, the play remains consistently comical, and Shaw deliberately chooses an anticlimactic resolution to the hothouse tensions built up in the play. The "real performance" of apocalyptic catastrophe does not take place, and we are left with scenes of a *praeludium*. The final scene has the character of an episode of sexual play in which moments of intense excitement are experienced but in which consummation is withheld. The excitement dies, and Beethoven moves over for Ivor Novello.

In some ways *Heartbreak House* could be seen as expressive of frustration on Shaw's part. The political causes for which he had fought were, temporarily at least, swept aside by the *force majeur* of a great war between imperial foes. His pamphlet "Common Sense about the War" did nothing to alter the course of events and succeeded in bringing down on his head an enormous amount of hostile invective, as well as social ostracism. His personal experiences in the realms of love and sex before the war must have continued to influence him. It is not difficult, however, to imagine that the act of writing the play would have had a considerable cathartic effect for Shaw in relation to these experiences. The self-delighting artistry of the work, its exuberant comedy and pungent satire, its masterful organization of extraordinarily complex dramatic materials all suggest a stance of gaiety and poise rather than defeat and disappointment.

Appendix: Select Checklist of Major U.K. and North American Productions, 1920–1992

1920   Garrick Theater, New York: Theater Guild
     Cast: Captain Shotover (Albert Perry)
                      Ellie Dunn (Elizabeth Risdon)
                      Hesione Hushabye (Effie Shannon)
                      Lady Utterword (Lucille Watson)
                      Hector Hushabye (Fred Eric)
                      Boss Mangan (Dudley Digges)
                      Mazzini Dunn (Erskine Sanford)
                      Nurse Guinness (Helen Westley)
                      Randall Utterword (Ralph Roeder)
                      The Burglar (Henry Travers)
     Director: Dudley Digges
     Designer: Lee Simonson

1921   Royal Court Theatre, London
     Cast: Captain Shotover (Brember Wills)
                      Ellie Dunn (Ellen O'Malley)
                      Hesione Hushabye (Mary Grey)
                      Lady Utterword (Edith Evans)
                      Hector Hushabye (James Dale)
                      Boss Mangan (Alfred Clark)
                      Mazzini Dunn (H. O. Nicholson)
                      Nurse Guinness (Lilian Talbot)

Randall Utterword (Eric Maturin)
The Burglar (Charles Groves)
Directors: George Bernard Shaw and J. B. Fagan
Designer: J. B. Fagan

1923   Birmingham Repertory Theatre, Birmingham, England
    Cast: Captain Shotover (Cedric Hardwicke)
            Ellie Dunn (Eileen Beldon)
            Hesione Hushabye (Margaret Chatwin)
            Lady Utterword (Evelyn Hope)
            Hector Hushabye (Scott Sunderland)
            Boss Mangan (Melville Cooper)
            Mazzini Dunn (Wallace Evennett)
            Nurse Guinness (Isabel Thornton)
            Randall Utterword (Colin Keith-Johnston)
            The Burglar (Paul Smythe)
    Director: H. K. Ayliff
    Designer: Paul Shelving

1932   Queen's Theatre, London
    Cast: Captain Shotover (Cedric Hardwicke)
            Ellie Dunn (Eileen Beldon)
            Hesione Hushabye (Margaret Chatwin)
            Lady Utterword (Edith Evans)
            Hector Hushabye (Leon Quartermayne)
            Boss Mangan (Wilfred Lawson)
            Mazzini Dunn (O. B. Clarence)
            Nurse Guinness (Isabel Thornton)
            Randall Utterword (Ballard Berkeley)
            The Burglar (Charles Groves)
    Director: H. K. Ayliff
    Designer: Paul Shelving

1937   Westminster Theatre, London
    Cast: Captain Shotover (Cecil Trouncer)
            Ellie Dunn (Margaret Hood)

Hesione Hushabye (Mary Grey)
Lady Utterword (Agnes Lauchlan)
Hector Hushabye (Alan Napier)
Boss Mangan (Mark Dignam)
Mazzini Dunn (Richard Goolden)
Nurse Guinness (Dora Gregory)
Randall Utterword (John Boddington)
The Burglar (Philip Godfrey)
Director: Michael MacOwen
Designer: Peter Goffin

1938   Mercury Theater, New York
Cast: Captain Shotover (Orson Welles)
Ellie Dunn (Geraldine Fitzgerald)
Hesione Hushabye (Mady Christians)
Lady Utterword (Phyllis Joyce)
Hector Hushabye (Vincent Price)
Boss Mangan (George Coulouris)
Mazzini Dunn (Erskine Sanford)
Nurse Guinness (Brenda Forbes)
Randall Utterword (John Hoysradt)
The Burglar (Eustace Wyatt)
Director: Orson Welles
Designer: John Koenig

1943   Cambridge Theatre, London
Cast: Captain Shotover (Robert Donat)
Ellie Dunn (Deborah Kerr)
Hesione Hushabye (Edith Evans)
Lady Utterword (Isabel Jeans)
Hector Hushabye (Vernon Kelso)
Boss Mangan (George Merritt)
Mazzini Dunn (J. H. Roberts)
Nurse Guinness (Amy Veness)
Randall Utterword (Francis Lister)
The Burglar (Philip Godfrey)

Director: John Burrell
Designer: Michael Relph
Costumes: Cecil Beaton

1950   Arts Club Theatre, London
  Cast: Captain Shotover (Walter Fitzgerald)
                Ellie Dunn (Jenny Laird)
                Hesione Hushabye (Catherine Lacey)
                Lady Utterword (Patricia Jessel)
                Hector Hushabye (Alan Judd)
                Boss Mangan (Duncan Lewis)
                Mazzini Dunn (Hugh Pryce)
                Nurse Guinness (Empsie Bowman)
                Randall Utterword (Anthony Marlowe)
                The Burglar (Howard Lamb)
  Director: John Fernald
  Designer: Ronald Brown

1959   Billy Rose Theater, New York
  Cast: Captain Shotover (Maurice Evans)
                Ellie Dunn (Diane Cilento)
                Hesione Hushabye (Diana Wynyard)
                Lady Utterword (Pamela Brown)
                Hector Hushabye (Dennis Price)
                Boss Mangan (Sam Levene)
                Mazzini Dunn (Alan Webb)
                Nurse Guinness (Jane Rose)
                Randall Utterword (Patrick Horgan)
                The Burglar (Sorrell Booke)
  Producers: Maurice Evans and Robert L. Joseph
  Director: Harold Clurman
  Designer: Ben Edwards

1961   Wyndham's Theatre, London: Oxford Playhouse
  Cast: Captain Shotover (Roger Livesey)
                Ellie Dunn (Perlita Neilson)

Hesione Hushabye (Judy Campbell)
Lady Utterword (Dulcie Gray)
Hector Hushabye (Michael Denison)
Boss Mangan (George Benson)
Mazzini Dunn (Donald Eccles)
Nurse Guinness (Joan Young)
Randall Utterword (Barry Sinclair)
The Burglar (Ken Wynne)
Director: Frank Hauser
Designer: Pauline Whitehouse

1967   Lyric Theatre, London: Chichester Festival
  Cast: Captain Shotover (John Clements)
Ellie Dunn (Sarah Badel)
Hesione Hushabye (Irene Worth)
Lady Utterword (Diana Churchill)
Hector Hushabye (Michael Aldridge)
Boss Mangan (Bill Fraser)
Mazzini Dunn (David Bird)
Nurse Guinness (Doris Hare)
Randall Utterword (John Humphry)
The Burglar (Carl Bernard)
Director: John Clements
Designer: Peter Rice

1968   Court House Theater, Niagara-on-the-Lake, Ontario: Shaw
Festival
  Cast: Captain Shotover (Tony Van Bridge)
Ellie Dunn (Diana Leblanc)
Hesione Hushabye (Jessica Tandy)
Lady Utterword (Frances Hyland)
Hector Hushabye (Paxton Whitehead)
Boss Mangan (Bill Fraser)
Mazzini Dunn (Patrick Boxill)
Nurse Guinness (Eleanor Beecroft)
Randall Utterword (James Valentine)

The Burglar (Kenneth Wickes)
Director: Val Gielgud
Designer: Maurice Strike

1975 National Theatre at the Old Vic, London
Cast: Captain Shotover (Colin Blakely)
Ellie Dunn (Kate Nelligan)
Hesione Hushabye (Eileen Atkins)
Lady Utterword (Anna Massey)
Hector Hushabye (Graham Crowden)
Boss Mangan (Paul Rogers)
Mazzini Dunn (Alan MacNaughtan)
Nurse Guinness (Patience Collier)
Randall Utterword (Edward de Souza)
The Burglar (Harry Lomax)
Director: John Schlesinger
Designer: Michael Annals

1975 Bristol Old Vic, Bristol, England
Cast: Captain Shotover (John Robinson)
Ellie Dunn (Joanna Van Gyseghen)
Hesione Hushabye (Barbara Jefford)
Lady Utterword (Moira Redmond)
Hector Hushabye (Basil Hoskins)
Boss Mangan (Harold Innocent)
Mazzini Dunn (Michael Rothwell)
Nurse Guinness (June Barrie)
Randall Utterword (Edgar Wreford)
The Burglar (Richard Mathews)
Director: John Tydeman
Designer: Roger Andrews

1976 Arena Stage, Washington D.C.
Cast: Captain Shotover (Robert Pastena)
Ellie Dunn (Dianne Wiest)

> Hesione Hushabye (Carolyn Coates)
> Lady Utterword (Barbara Caruso)
> Hector Hushabye (Jack Byland)
> Boss Mangan (Howard Witt)
> Mazzini Dunn (Max Wright)
> Nurse Guinness (Grayce Grant)
> Randall Utterword (Jeffrey Jones)
> The Burglar (Terrence Currier)

Director: John Pasquin
Designer: Santo Loquasto

1980   Malvern Festival Theatre, Malvern, England
    Cast: Captain Shotover (Anthony Quayle)
        Ellie Dunn (Mel Martin)
        Hesione Hushabye (Barbara Murray)
        Lady Utterword (Honor Blackman)
        Hector Hushabye (Patrick Cargill)
        Boss Mangan (Paul Hardwick)
        Mazzini Dunn (Ken Wynne)
        Nurse Guinness (Elizabeth Hunt)
        Randall Utterword (John Quentin)
        The Burglar (Robert Aldous)
    Director: Clifford Williams
    Designer: John Gunter

1983   Theatre Royal, London: Royal Shakespeare Company
    Cast: Captain Shotover (Rex Harrison)
        Ellie Dunn (Mel Martin)
        Hesione Hushabye (Diana Rigg)
        Lady Utterword (Rosemary Harris)
        Hector Hushabye (Paxton Whitehead)
        Boss Mangan (Frank Middlemass)
        Mazzini Dunn (Paul Curran)
        Nurse Guinness (Doris Hare)
        Randall Utterword (Simon Ward)

The Burglar (Charles Lloyd Pack)
Director: John Dexter
Designer: Jocelyn Herbert

1983   Circle in the Square Theater, New York
    Cast: Captain Shotover (Rex Harrison)
            Ellie Dunn (Amy Irving)
            Hesione Hushabye (Rosemary Harris)
            Lady Utterword (Dana Ivey)
            Hector Hushabye (Stephen McHattie)
            Boss Mangan (Philip Bosco)
            Mazzini Dunn (William Prince)
            Nurse Guinness (Jan Minor)
            Randall Utterword (Bill Moor)
    Director: Anthony Page
    Designer: Marjorie Bradley Kellogg

1985   Citizens' Theatre, Glasgow
    Cast: Captain Shotover (Robert David MacDonald)
            Ellie Dunn (Yolanda Vasquez)
            Hesione Hushabye (Jill Spurrier)
            Lady Utterword (Jane Bertish)
            Hector Hushabye (Robert Gwilym)
            Boss Mangan (Patrick Hannway)
            Mazzini Dunn (Giles Havergal)
            Nurse Guinness (Ida Schuster)
            Randall Utterword (Rupert Everett)
            The Burglar (Keith Casburn)
    Director: Philip Prowse
    Designer: Philip Prowse

1992   Theatre Royal, London
    Cast: Captain Shotover (Paul Scofield)
            Ellie Dunn (Imogen Stubbs)
            Hesione Hushabye (Vanessa Redgrave)
            Lady Utterword (Felicity Kendal)

Appendix

Hector Hushabye (Daniel Massey)
Boss Mangan (David Calder)
Mazzini Dunn (Oliver Ford Davies)
Nurse Guinness (Peggy Marshall)
Randall Utterword (Shaun Scott)
The Burglar (Joe Melia)
Director: Trevor Nunn
Designer: William Dudley

Notes

1. Revolution and Struggle

1. August Strindberg, Preface to *Miss Julie*, in *August Strindberg: The Plays*, rev. ed., trans. Michael Meyer (London: Secker & Warburg, 1975), 2: 101.

2. Martin Meisel, *Shaw and the Nineteenth-Century Theater* (Princeton, N.J.: Princeton University Press, 1963), 315–16.

3. *Bernard Shaw: Collected Letters*, ed. Dan H. Laurence (London, Sydney, and Toronto: Max Reinhardt, 1965–88), 3:740–41; hereafter cited in text as *Letters*.

4. Eric Bentley, *Bernard Shaw* (1947, rev. 1957; Methuen & Co., 1967), 96.

5. This date is recorded in a letter from Shaw to Mrs. Patrick Campbell of 14 May 1916. In a "morose" mood, he recorded his early difficulties with the play as follows: "I cant write: nothing comes off but screeds for the papers, mostly about this blasted war. I am old and finished. I, who once wrote whole plays *d'un seul trait*, am creeping through a new one (to prevent myself from crying) at odd moments, two or three speeches at a time. I dont know what its about. I began it on the 4th March: and I have hardly come to the beginning of the first scene yet" (*Bernard Shaw and Mrs. Patrick Campbell: Their Correspondence*, ed. Alan Dent [London: Victor Gollancz, 1952], 209; hereafter cited in text as *Correspondence*).

6. In her reply to this letter, on 15 May 1940, Virginia Woolf said that the falling in love had not been "one sided" and that *Heartbreak House* was her favorite of Shaw's works (*Letters*, 4:558).

7. See Stanley Weintraub, *Journey to Heartbreak: The Crucible Years of Bernard Shaw, 1914–1918* (New York: Weybright & Talley, 1971), 165; hereafter cited in text.

2. The Importance of *Heartbreak House*

1. Anonymous review ("The New Shaw Play"), in the Billy Rose Theatre Collection, Lincoln Center, New York.

2. Richard Watts, Jr., review, *New York Post*, 19 October 1959.

3. See Desmond MacCarthy, *Shaw* (London: MacGibbon & Kee, 1951), 144; hereafter cited in text.

3. Critical Reception

1. See T. F. Evans, *Shaw: The Critical Heritage* (London, Henley, and Boston: Routledge & Kegan Paul, 1976), 236, 242; hereafter cited in text.

2. Sydney W. Carroll, *Sunday Times*, 23 October 1921.

3. Desmond MacCarthy, *New Statesman*, 29 October 1921; reprinted in his *Shaw*.

4. Desmond MacCarthy, *New Statesman*, 3 April 1943; reprinted in his *Shaw*.

5. E. M. W., review, *Birmingham Evening Despatch*, 17 April 1923.

6. See Daniel C. Gerould, "Soviet Shaw, Slavic Shaw: Moscow, 1967," *Shaw Review* 10 (September 1967): 84–92.

7. Jeremy Kingston, review, *Plays and Players* 22, no. 7 (April 1975): 20.

8. The full cast for this production is listed in the Appendix.

9. Mary McCarthy, *Sights and Spectacles, 1937–1958* (London: Heinemann, 1959), 38.

10. Edmund Wilson, *The Triple Thinkers* (Harmondsworth: Penguin, 1962), 213.

11. F. P. W. McDowell, "Technique, Symbol, and Theme in *Heartbreak House*," *PMLA* 68, no. 3 (1953): 335–56.

12. See Meisel, 314–15; Michael W. Kaufman, "The Dissonance of Dialetic: Shaw's *Heartbreak House*," *Shaw Review* 13, no. 1 (January 1970): 2–9.

13. C. B. Purdom, *A Guide to the Plays of Bernard Shaw* (London: Methuen, 1963), 261.

14. Margery M. Morgan, *The Shavian Playground: An Exploration of the Art of Bernard Shaw* (London: Methuen, 1972).

15. Peter Ure, "Master and Pupil in Bernard Shaw," *Essays in Criticism* 19, no. 2 (1969): 135. Compare J. C. Trewin: "Without accepting this idea [that the whole play is Ellie's dream], one does know that *Heartbreak House* can have the extravagant dimensions of a dream, a strangeness that is over the edge of the world" ("On Top of the World," review of 1975 National Theatre revival, *Illustrated London News*, May 1975).

Notes

16. Charles A. Carpenter, *Bernard Shaw and the Art of Destroying Ideals* (Madison: University of Wisconsin Press, 1969); Louis Crompton, *Shaw the Dramatist* (Lincoln: University of Nebraska Press, 1969); A. M. Gibbs, *Shaw* (Edinburgh: Oliver & Boyd, 1969); Elsie B. Adams, *Bernard Shaw and the Aesthetes* (Columbus: Ohio State University Press, 1971); Morgan, *The Shavian Playground*; Charles A. Berst, *Bernard Shaw and the Art of Drama* (Urbana: University of Illinois Press, 1973); Maurice J. Valency, *The Cart and the Trumpet: The Plays of Bernard Shaw* (New York: Oxford University Press, 1973); J. L. Wisenthal, *The Marriage of Contraries: Bernard Shaw's Middle Plays* (Cambridge: Harvard University Press, 1974); Alfred Turco, *Shaw's Moral Vision* (Ithaca, N.Y.: Cornell University Press, 1976); R. F. Whitman, *Shaw and the Play of Ideas* (Ithaca, N.Y.: Cornell University Press, 1977). All hereafter cited in text.

17. Stark Young, "Heartbreak Houses," in *George Bernard Shaw: A Critical Survey*, ed. Louis Kronenberger (Cleveland and New York: World Publishing Co., 1953), 233.

18. J. I. M. Stewart, *Eight Modern Writers* (Oxford: Oxford University Press, 1963), 169–74; Homer E. Woodbridge, *George Bernard Shaw, Creative Artist* (Carbondale: Southern Illinois University Press, 1963), 106–107; Nicholas Grene, *Bernard Shaw: A Critical View* (London: Macmillan, 1984), 114–31. All hereafter cited in text.

19. These judicious cuts, which save time at a crucial phase, are not indicated in any current edition and have been edited from the text of the relevant letter printed in *Letters*, 3:738–39. The full text of Shaw's letter of 20 October 1921 instructing the producer, J. B. Fagan, to make the cuts is printed in Stanley Weintraub, *The Portable Bernard Shaw* (Harmondsworth: Penguin, 1977), 578–80.

20. Anne Wright, *Literature of Crisis, 1910–1922* (London: Macmillan, 1984), and "Shaw's Burglars: *Heartbreak House* and *Too True to Be Good*," *Shaw Review* 23, no. 1 (1980): 2–10; hereafter cited in text.

21. See Frank Kermode, *The Sense of an Ending* (New York: Oxford University Press, 1967), chapter 4.

22. E. M. Forster, *Howards End* (Harmondsworth: Penguin, 1975), 178.

23. The theme of childishness is explored in relation to J. M. Barrie's portrayal of the world of childhood in *Peter Pan and Wendy* in a perceptive essay by Axel Kruse, "Bernard Shaw's *Heartbreak House*: The War in 'Neverland,'" *Sydney Studies in English* 13 (1987–88): 100–19.

4. A Chamber of Echoes

1. Shaw's description, in the *Saturday Review*, 30 April 1898. See *Our Theatres in the Nineties by Bernard Shaw* (London: Constable, 1932), 3:373; hereafter cited in text as *Theatres*.

2. Philip was the son of Sir Edward Burne-Jones and one of Mrs. Pat's admirers. His 1897 painting, the original of which is now apparently lost, is discussed and described by Margot Peters in *Mrs. Pat: The Life of Mrs. Patrick Campbell* (London: Hamish Hamilton, 1985): "It showed a beautiful woman with cascading black hair in a clinging nightdress, astride a man collapsed across a bed. The woman's face is intent and joyful; her teeth are long and sharp" (142–43). Shaw's allusion to this painting and Stella Campbell in *Heartbreak House* was noted by Louis Crompton in his *Shaw the Dramatist*, 158.

3. The allusions to Peter Pan and Wendy in the Shaw–Campbell correspondence, and the connections with *Heartbreak House*, are explored in Axel Kruse's essay "Bernard Shaw's *Heartbreak House*: The War in 'Neverland.'"

4. This description occurs in a highly charged passage of dialogue in act 2 of *The Father*, in which Laura expresses her revulsion at her dual role of being both the mother and the mistress of the captain, and which concludes with her cruel dismissal of him as "no longer needed." See *August Strindberg: The Plays*, 1:68–71.

5. Preface to the 1913 edition of *The Quintessence of Ibsenism*, in *Shaw and Ibsen: Bernard Shaw's "The Quintessence of Ibsenism" and Related Writings*, ed. J. L. Wisenthal (Toronto, Buffalo, and London: University of Toronto Press, 1979), 101–102; hereafter cited in text as *Shaw and Ibsen*.

6. Strindberg to Charles de Casenove, 26 June 1892. Cited in Michael Meyer, *Strindberg: A Biography* (Oxford and New York: Oxford University Press, 1987), 246.

7. Nina Auerbach, *Woman and the Demon: The Life of a Victorian Myth* (Cambridge, Mass., and London: Harvard University Press, 1982); hereafter cited in text.

8. This is the title her subjects use for the sorceress-ruler, Ayesha, in Rider Haggard's *She*, comically employed by John Mortimer for Rumpole's mutterings about his wife, Hilda, in *Rumpole of the Bailey*.

9. Several of these statements are gathered in section 6, "Shaw on Feminist Issues," of *Fabian Feminist: Bernard Shaw and Woman*, ed. Rodelle Weintraub (University Park and London: Pennsylvania State University Press, 1977), 227–59. In her essay "Feminism and Female Stereotypes in Shaw," in the volume just cited, Elsie B. Adams argues that we need to make "a clear distinction between Shaw's traditional treatment of women in the plays and his feminist politics" (*Fabian Feminist*, 161). Although there is a need in a number of instances to make this distinction, Adams seems to me to overstate the case for saying that Shaw's female characters are out of line with his "feminist politics."

10. As Anne Wright says in *Literature of Crisis, 1910–1922*, the men of *Heartbreak House* are "infantilised" by the women (93).

11. I am indebted in the following discussion of the Shaw–Cotterill relationship to Dan H. Laurence's account in *Letters*, 2:562–63, but I consider that the relationship was a more significant episode in Shaw's life than Laurence suggests. Cotterill's autobiographical writings, *An Account* (1916) and *Form of Diary* (1939), and her play, *A Professional Socialist* (1908), indicate her remarkable literary ability. The second volume of *An Account* is dedicated "To Bernard Shaw whom I love."

12. In a letter written to John Wardrop on 3 September 1942, Shaw gave a further graphic glimpse of Erica's behavior: "If a man interested her she would walk into his house at any hour: mostly in the middle of the night; take possession of him as if his astonished and outraged wife did not exist; and be quite unconscious of any reason why she should not sleep with him and live in the house as long as she wanted to" (*Letters*, 4:637).

13. An allusion to *The Master Builder* in one of Shaw's letters to Erica indicates that she knew the play, and it is a reasonable guess that she would have been aware of this parallel. See *Letters*, 2:700.

14. Margot Peters, *Bernard Shaw and the Actresses* (Garden City, N.Y.: Doubleday, 1980), 405; hereafter cited in text.

15. "Mr. Shaw's Literary Morals," statement for the *Observer*, 11 January 1914, in *The Bodley Head Bernard Shaw*, 4:799. "My plays are full of pillage," Shaw says in the same statement, made in reply to a charge that he had stolen the plot of *Pygmalion* from Tobias Smollett's *Peregrine Pickle* (which he had not read).

16. John A. Bertolini identifies a pattern of reverse parallel in his discussion of the relation of Shaw's *Caesar and Cleopatra* with Shakespeare's *Antony and Cleopatra*, which exemplifies the principle referred to here. See *The Playwrighting Self of Bernard Shaw* (Carbondale and Edwardsville: Southern Illinois University Press, 1991), 9–26.

17. Charles Dickens, *David Copperfield* (Harmondsworth: Penguin, 1966), 79, 82. Some of the Dickensian echoes I discuss later were noted by Martin Quinn in his essay "The Dickensian Presence in *Heartbreak House*," *Shaw Review* 20, no. 3 (1977): 119–25. But Quinn does not observe the transformations that occur in Shaw's handling of Dickensian themes and motifs.

18. Charles Dickens, *Dombey and Son* (Harmondsworth: Penguin, 1970), 88–89; hereafter cited in text as *DS*.

19. Tony Tanner, *Jane Austen* (London: Macmillan, 1986), 224.

20. This remark, by a Mr. Earle Welby, is quoted by James Agate in a review of the 1932 revival of *Heartbreak House* at the Queen's Theatre (*Sunday Times*, 25 April 1932).

21. Charles Dickens, *Bleak House* (Harmondsworth: Penguin, 1971), 299; hereafter cited in text as *BH*. Shaw refers to the "arrogant numskull" Dedlock in the draft of an essay, "From Dickens to Ibsen," written in 1889.

See Dan H. Laurence and Martin Quinn, *Shaw on Dickens* (New York: Frederick Ungar, 1985), 20.

22. Dickens alludes here to the telling of the story of the flood and Noah's ark in Matthew 24:38ff.

23. Shaw coined this term in his Preface to *Three Plays for Puritans* (1901), in *The Bodley Head Bernard Shaw*, 2:41.

24. Preface to *Man and Superman*, in *The Bodley Head Bernard Shaw*, 2: 520. Dickens is coupled with Shakespeare in this charge.

25. Shaw's awareness of this connection is shown in a letter to St. John Ervine of 23 October 1921: "Hector declaims all through like him of Troy" (*Letters*, 3:743). Hector's pseudonym, Marcus Darnley, is possibly derived in part from that of Henry Stuart, Lord Darnley (1546?–67), the second husband of Mary Queen of Scots. Darnley was a handsome and dashing but vain and decadent young aristocrat with whom Mary became infatuated. They entered into a politically unwise marriage in 1565. Mary was several years older than Darnley, and a contemporary historian remarks on the maternal nature of her feelings for him, which resemble Hesione's for Hector: "She was to him not only a loyal Prince, a loving and dear wife, but a most careful and tender Mother withal" (John Leslie, bishop of Ross, cited in Antonia Fraser, *Mary Queen of Scots* [London: Methuen, 1969], 291). The sensational circumstances of Darnley's murder may have been in Shaw's mind when he was writing the end of *Heartbreak House*. On the 10 February 1567 the young king was the intended victim of an enormous explosion of gunpowder that reduced the house in which he had been staying to rubble. After the botched gunpowder plot, his assailants strangled Darnley and his servant as they were trying to escape.

26. In his note to this passage in the Arden edition of *King Lear*, Kenneth Muir cites Edward Jordan, *A Brief Discourse of a Disease Called the Suffocation of the Mother*, 1605: "This disease is called by diverse names amongst our authors, *Passio Hysterica, Suffocatio Priefocatio, and Strangulatus uteri, Caducus Matricis*, i.e. in English, the Mother or the Suffocation of the Mother, because, most commonly, it takes them with choking in the throat; and it is an affect of the mother or wombe, wherein the principal parts of the bodie by consent do suffer diversely according to the diversitie of the causes and diseases wherewith the matrix is offended" (Kenneth Muir, ed., *King Lear*, rev. ed. [London: Methuen, 1972], 81). Coppelia Kahn shows the significance of this passage and of ideas about the mother and maternal nurture in the play in "The Absent Mother in *King Lear*," in *Rewriting the Renaissance: The Discourses of Sexual Difference in Early Modern Europe*, ed. Margaret W. Ferguson, Maureen Quilligan, and Nancy J. Vickers (Chicago and London: University of Chicago Press, 1986), 33–49. I am indebted to Kahn's discussion of Lear's simultaneous craving for maternal tenderness from his daughters and fear about the usurpation of his manhood by "womanish" feelings.

27. The Omphale legend comes prominently into play toward the end of Strindberg's *The Father*, as the Captain nears his final downfall at the hands of Laura and the Nurse.

28. *The Cherry Orchard* was presented by the Stage Society at the Aldwych Theatre on 28 May 1911. It was not well received, but Shaw was deeply impressed by Chekhov's dramatic artistry; later in 1911 he reported to George Moore, with reference to the Stage Society production, that "an exquisite play by Tchekoff was actually hissed" (*Letters*, 3:52–53).

29. Anton Chekhov, *The Cherry Orchard*, in *Plays: Anton Chekhov*, trans. Elisaveta Fen (Harmondsworth: Penguin, 1959), 358; hereafter cited in text as CO.

30. Anton Chekhov, *Uncle Vanya*, in *Plays: Anton Chekhov*, 205; hereafter cited in text as UV.

31. The motif of suffocation recurs in *Uncle Vanya*. Vanya himself feels "suffocated" by the thought that his life has been "irretrievably lost" (*UV*, 205), and the doctor, Astrov, says that he could not stand being in the Serebriakov house for a month: "I should be suffocated in this atmosphere" (*UV*, 210).

32. Michael Billington, in a review of a London production of *Uncle Vanya*, "Missing the Magic," *Guardian Weekly*, week ending 1 September 1991, 26.

33. *Uncle Vanya* (1899) predates *Man and Superman* (1901–1903), but Shaw's awareness of Chekhov's work apparently dates from 1905. See Shaw's letter to Laurence Irving, 25 October 1905: "I hear that there are several dramas extant by Whatshisname (Tchekoff, or something like that)—the late Russian novelist who wrote The Black Monk &c" (*Letters*, 2:569).

34. John Tulloch argues persuasively against this tradition of Chekhovian criticism in his *Chekhov: A Structuralist Study* (London: Macmillan, 1980).

5. Discontinuities

1. Michael W. Kaufman discusses this analogy, linking it to thematic concerns in the play, in his article "The Dissonance of Dialectic: Shaw's *Heartbreak House*," 2–9.

2. For comparison with Strindberg's play, see Margery M. Morgan's chapter "*Heartbreak House*: Shaw's Dream Play" in her *The Shavian Playground*, 200–20. Richard Watts, Jr., in a review of a 1938 production of *Heartbreak House* at the Mercury Theater in New York, described Ellie as "a sort of wandering Alice in Shaw's Wonderland" (*New York Herald Tribune*, 30 April 1938). James Woodfield extends this comparison in "Ellie in Wonderland: Dream and Madness in *Heartbreak House*," *English Studies in Canada* 11, no. 3 (1985): 334–45.

3. *Tristan and Isolde* is alluded to by Hesione in act 2 of *Heartbreak House* (140).

4. The comparison supplies the play's most explicit allusion to *Alice in Wonderland*. The motifs of tea making and serving in the quirky atmosphere of act 1 may also be an echo of the Mad Hatter's tea party.

5. See Henry Donaghy, *James Clarence Mangan* (New York: Twayne, 1974), 27. Shaw probably had the poet in mind when he named the character in *Heartbreak House*.

6. D. H. Lawrence, letter to Edward Garnett, 5 June 1914, in *The Letters of D. H. Lawrence*, ed. James T. Boulton et al. (Cambridge: Cambridge University Press, 1979–), 2:183; hereafter cited in text as Lawrence.

7. "R.A.D.A. Pass Shavian Test," unsigned newspaper review of a production at the Vanbrugh Theatre, London, in 1959 (Theatre Museum, Covent Garden).

6. Symbolism and the Supernatural

1. The source is Hesketh Pearson, *Bernard Shaw: Life and Personality* (London: Collins, 1950), 115; quoted in Arthur H. Nethercot, *The First Five Lives of Annie Besant* (London: Rupert Hart-Davis, 1961), 296.

2. A copy of H. P. Blavatsky's *The Secret Doctrine: The Synthesis of Science, Religion, and Philosophy* (London: Theosophical Publishing Co., 1888) was sent to Shaw for review in *The Star* in 1889. See *Bernard Shaw: The Diaries, 1885–1897*, ed. Stanley Weintraub (University Park and London: Pennsylvania State University Press, 1986), 1:455. Although he passed the reviewing task on to his friend Annie Besant, who shortly thereafter became a convert to Theosophy, it seems clear from the echoes in his work that Shaw was quite well acquainted with the ideas conveyed in Blavatsky's work. Charlotte Shaw was deeply interested in Indian mysticism and would probably have enlarged Shaw's earlier knowledge of the subject.

3. Blavatsky, *The Secret Doctrine*, 1:40; hereafter cited in text. This passage contains some remarkable resemblances to ideas about creative evolution and heaven as the home of the masters of reality, which Shaw was to develop later in *Man and Superman, Back to Methuselah*, and other writings.

4. See Iona and Peter Opie, *The Classic Fairy Tales* (London: Oxford University Press, 1974), 199–205.

5. A similar ambiguity is present in the presentation of the other child heroine with whom Ellie has been compared, Alice in Wonderland. At times she is a little-girl victim threatened by such dangerous personages as the Queen; at other times, however, she herself is a threatening, invasive figure among the creatures of Wonderland, and the Pigeon thinks she is a serpent.

7. Preludes of Apocalypse

1. Spender made this comment in the course of a 1988 BBC television panel discussion, directed by David Heycock and entitled "Eliot and After."

2. H. J. Schonfield, *Secrets of the Dead Sea Scrolls: Studies towards Their Solution* (London: Valentine, Mitchell, 1956), 112, 113, cited in D. S. Russell, *The Method and Message of Jewish Apocalyptic, 200* B.C.–A.D. *100* (Philadelphia: Westminster Press, 1964), 263–64.

3. *The Black Girl in Search of God: And Some Lesser Tales* (Harmondsworth: Penguin, 1946), 22.

4. William Wordsworth, *The Prelude*, book 6, ll. 633–39.

5. *Biographia Literaria; or, Biographical Sketches of My Literary Life and Opinions*, ed. James Engell and W. Jackson Bate (London: Routledge & Kegan Paul; Princeton, N.J.: Princeton University Press, 1983), no. 7 of *The Collected Works of Samuel Taylor Coleridge*, ed. K. Coburn (1983–), 1:304. Blake's *The Marriage of Heaven and Hell* repeatedly plays with apocalyptic paradox, and the verses accompanying Plate 14 of that work declare that "the ancient tradition that the world will be consumed in fire at the end of six thousand years is true, as I have heard from Hell." The collapse of opposites is an essential theme of this passage, in which Blake ingeniously imagines himself as some kind of infernal lithographer: "The notion that man has a body distinct from his soul is to be expunged; this I shall do, by printing in the infernal method, by corrosives, which in Hell are salutary and medicinal, melting apparent surfaces away, and displaying the infinite which was hid. . . . If the doors of perception were cleansed every thing would appear to man as it is, infinite." Ellie Dunn's preaching to Shotover that "we know now that the soul is the body, and the body the soul" (145) seems to echo this and similar utterances in *The Marriage of Heaven and Hell*.

6. Thomas J. J. Altizer, *History as Apocalypse* (Albany: State University of New York Press, 1985), 170.

7. The fact that the works were being written almost simultaneously rules out the possibility of any direct interaction between the two texts, although it is not impossible that Lawrence knew of Shaw's ideas about evolution as expounded in *Man and Superman*.

8. Frank Kermode, "Lawrence and the Apocalyptic Types," in *D. H. Lawrence: The Rainbow and Women in Love: A Casebook*, ed. Colin Clarke (London: Macmillan, 1969), 203–18.

9. D. H. Lawrence, *Kangaroo* (Harmondsworth: Penguin, 1950), 240.

10. Lawrence, 2:331, cited in Keith Sagar, *D. H. Lawrence: Life into Art* (Athens: University of Georgia Press, 1985), 155.

11. "Bernard Shaw on *Heartbreak House*," London *Sunday Herald*, 23 October 1921, in *The Bodley Head Bernard Shaw*, 5:184

12. D. H. Lawrence, *Women in Love* (Harmondsworth: Penguin, 1960), 65; hereafter cited in text as *WL*.

13. For an expansion of this idea, see *The Black Girl in Search of God*, 67.

14. I have written more fully about this subject in the essay "Shaw and Creative Evolution," in *Irish Writers and Religion*, ed. Robert Welch (Savage, Md.: Barnes & Noble Books, 1992), 75–88.

15. Ursula too—more benevolently, though she herself is seen as "demoniacal" (*WL*, 142)—adopts a maternal role toward her lovers. She "saw her men as sons, pitied their yearning and admired their courage, and wondered over them as a mother wonders over her child" (*WL*, 296).

16. Other critics who have commented on the anticlimactic end of the play—the nonarrival of the apocalyptic moment—include Alfred J. Turco, Jr., and David J. Gordon. Turco sees Hector's turning on of the lights to invite destruction as "the vain finale of a *Götterdämmerung* in which Valhalla cannot catch fire" and argues that "the conclusion may be seen as an anticlimax in which nothing happens, really" (*Shaw's Moral Vision: The Self and Salvation* [Ithaca, N.Y., and London: Cornell University Press, 1976], 262–63). Gordon aptly describes the play as a "baffled apocalypse" (*Bernard Shaw and the Comic Sublime* [London: Macmillan, 1990], 163).

17. Matthew 24:38–39. The resemblance of the biblical story is noted by Martin Meisel in "Shaw and the Revolution," in *Shaw: Seven Critical Essays*, ed. Norman Rosenblood (Toronto: University of Toronto Press, 1971), 130. In this essay Meisel also perceptively notes how the end of *Heartbreak House* and the fate of Mangan and the Burglar in relation to that of the other characters parallels another passage of apocalyptic writing in the Gospels: "who ever shall seek to save his life shall lose it; and whoever shall lose his life shall preserve it" (Luke 17:33). I disagree, however, with Meisel when he says "Apocalypse—the raising of hell to heaven by high explosives—does come at last in *Heartbreak House*." This seems to be precisely what does not happen.

18. Devonport's resignation and replacement by Lord Rhondda is recorded in Malcolm Thomson, *David Lloyd George: The Official Biography* (London: Hutchinson & Co., 1948), 266–67. Beatrice Webb scathingly commented in her diary entry for 22 February 1917 on the appointments of interested parties, including the "egregious Devonport" to Lloyd George's War Ministry (*The Diary of Beatrice Webb*, ed. Norman and Jean Mackenzie [London: Virago Press, 1984], 3:276–77). Devonport had made himself extremely unpopular with workers and left-wing sympathizers before the war because of his use of scab labor to break a serious dock strike in the summer of 1912, in his capacity then as chairman of the Port of London Authority.

Notes

19. A. M. Gibbs, *The Art and Mind of Shaw: Essays in Criticism* (London: Macmillan, 1983), 188.

20. James Clarence Mangan, *Poems*, ed. John Mitchel (New York: P. M. Haverty, 1859), 453. See also Gibbs, *The Art and Mind of Shaw*, 188.

21. Patricia Pugh, "Bernard Shaw, Imperialist," in *Shaw and Politics*, ed. T. F. Evans, *The Annual of Bernard Shaw Studies* (University Park: Pennsylvania State University Press, 1991), 11:97–118.

22. The latter point about the setting of the play is made by Axel Kruse in "Bernard Shaw's *Heartbreak House*: The War in 'Neverland,'" 107–108.

23. Angus Wilson, "The Artist as Your Enemy Is Your Only Friend," *Southern Review* (Australia) 2, no. 2 (1966): 113. Wilson's essay (originally delivered as a lecture as the Writers' Week of the 1966 Adelaide Festival of Arts) presents what is possibly the most incisive and succinct account to date of Shaw's significance as a writer who bridged the divide created in the mid-nineteenth century between "serious" and "popular" art. His comments in this essay about Shaw's works in relation to various English Renaissance plays that are "a mixture, as life is, of horror and laughter, of farce and tragedy at the same time" (112) are especially relevant to *Heartbreak House*.

24. Lois Parkinson Zamora, *Writing the Apocalypse: Historical Vision in Contemporary U.S. and Latin American Fiction* (Cambridge, New York, New Rochelle, Melbourne, and Sydney: Cambridge University Press, 1989), 2; hereafter cited in text.

25. The Burglar episode was the subject of disagreement between the directors of two productions of the play, both starring Rex Harrison, in 1983. John Dexter's London production preserved the Burglar. But when Anthony Page took the play to New York later that year, the Burglar was excised. Page's argument at the time—that the burglar detracts from the seriousness of the play—is, I believe, invalid. Dexter "considered the Burglar episode integral to *Heartbreak House*" (see Samuel G. Freedman, "Director's Cut Stirs Debate on Shaw Play," *New York Times*, 9 December 1983).

26. One of the "Maxims for Revolutionists" in the "Revolutionist's Handbook and Pocket Companion" appended to *Man and Superman* reads, "Property, said Proudhon, is theft. This is the only perfect truism that has been uttered on the subject" (2:787).

27. In Revelation the Apocalypse and Judgment Day are heralded by the sounding in sequence of seven trumpets by seven angels. There is a probable echo of this in the last scene of *King Lear*, in the successive sounding of trumpets before the entry of Edgar. Randall's flute playing parodies both the biblical and Shakespearean texts.

28. [David] Ivor Novello (1893–1951), composer, playwright, and actor, was born in Wales and won a singing scholarship to Magdalen College,

Oxford, at the age of 10. As the author of musical comedies and plays, in which he took leading roles himself, he became one of the most popular and successful men of the theater of his day. During World War I he played a prominent part in the entertainment of Allied troops. The copyright of "Keep the Home Fires Burning" was taken out in 1914 by Ascherberg, Hopwood, and Crew, Ltd. For lyrics and music see *The Ivor Novello Song Album* (New York: Chappell, 1988), 64–68.

29. As in the case of my Tasmanian-born father, John Frederick Lloyd Gibbs (1897–1949), who was severely wounded by shrapnel at Gallipoli in 1915.

30. For an account of this speech, "The Illusions of War," see R. Page Arnot, *Bernard Shaw and William Morris* (London: William Morris Society, 1957), 22–23; reprinted in *Shaw: Interviews and Recollections*, ed. A. M. Gibbs (London: Macmillan, 1990), 232–33.

31. I have pointed out elsewhere in this study that, for the most part, Shaw avoided specific reference to contemporary history in *Heartbreak House*. The playing of "Keep the Home Fires Burning" is the most explicit topical allusion in the play.

Selected Bibliography

Primary Works

Bernard Shaw: The Diaries, 1885–1897. Edited and annotated by Stanley Weintraub. University Park and London: Pennsylvania State University Press, 1985.

Bernard Shaw and Mrs. Patrick Campbell: Their Correspondence. Edited by Alan Dent. London: Victor Gollancz, 1952.

Bernard Shaw: Collected Letters. Edited by Dan H. Laurence. 4 vols. London, Sydney, and Toronto: Max Reinhardt, 1965–88.

The Bodley Head Bernard Shaw: Collected Plays and Their Prefaces. Edited by Dan. H. Laurence. 7 vols. London, Sydney, and Toronto: Max Reinhardt, The Bodley Head, 1970–74.

Bernard Shaw, Heartbreak House: A Facsimile of the Revised Typescript. Edited by Stanley Weintraub and Anne Wright. New York and London: Garland, 1981.

Bernard Shaw: Major Critical Essays. With an introduction by Michael Holroyd. Harmondsworth: Penguin, 1986.

Our Theatres in the Nineties by Bernard Shaw. 3 vols. London: Constable, 1932.

Shaw: An Autobiography. Selected from his writings by Stanley Weintraub. 2 vols. London: Max Reinhardt, 1970, 1971.

Shaw and Ibsen. Edited by J. L. Wisenthal. Toronto: University of Toronto Press, 1979.

Shaw on Dickens. Edited by Dan H. Laurence and Martin Quinn. New York: Ungar, 1984.

Shaw on Religion. Edited by Warren Sylvester Smith. London: Constable, 1967.

Shaw on Shakespeare. Edited by Edwin Wilson. New York: Dutton, 1961; London: Cassell, 1962.

Shaw on the Theater. Edited by E. J. West. New York: Hill & Wang, 1958.

The Religious Speeches of Bernard Shaw. Edited by Warren Sylvester Smith. University Park: Pennsylvania State University Press, 1963.

Secondary Works

Biography

Ervine, St. John. *Bernard Shaw: His Life, Work and Friends.* London: Constable, 1956.

Gibbs, A. M. *Bernard Shaw: Interviews and Recollections.* London: Macmillan, 1990.

Henderson, Archibald. *George Bernard Shaw: His Life and Works.* London: Hurst & Blackett; Cincinnati: Stewart & Kidd, 1911.

____. *Bernard Shaw: Playboy and Prophet.* New York and London: D. Appleton and Co., 1932.

____. *George Bernard Shaw: Man of the Century.* 2 vols. New York: Appleton-Century-Crofts, 1956.

Holroyd, Michael. *Shaw.* 4 vols. London: Chatto & Windus, 1988–92.

Peters, Margot. *Bernard Shaw and the Actresses.* Garden City, N.Y.: Doubleday, 1980.

Weintraub, Stanley. *Journey to Heartbreak: The Crucible Years of Bernard Shaw, 1914–1918.* New York: Weybright & Talley, 1971; London: Routledge & Kegan Paul, 1973.

Critical Studies

Bentley, Eric. *Bernard Shaw.* Norfolk, Conn.: New Directions Books, 1947; rev. ed., 1957. Pioneering study of Shaw as thinker and dramatist.

Berst, Charles A. *Bernard Shaw and the Art of Drama.* Urbana: University of Illinois Press, 1973. Focuses on aesthetic properties and thematic concerns of the plays.

Bertolini, John A. *The Playwrighting Self of George Bernard Shaw.* Carbondale and Edwardsville: Southern Illinois University Press, 1991. Analyzes the nature of Shaw's creative self and techniques as a playwright. Emphasizes the continuous sense of rivalry with Shakespeare.

Brustein, Robert. *The Theater of Revolt*. Boston: Little, Brown, 1964; London: Methuen, 1965. Includes discussion of *Heartbreak House*.

Crompton, Louis. *Shaw the Dramatist*. Lincoln: University of Nebraska Press, 1969. Critical study of the plays in relation to their intellectual, political, and social background.

Evans, T. F. *Shaw: The Critical Heritage*. London, Henley, and Boston: Routledge & Kegan Paul, 1976. Provides a general survey of the development of Shaw's reputation and an extensive selection of early notices and reviews of the plays.

Fromm, Harold. *Bernard Shaw and the Theater in the Nineties: A Study of Shaw's Dramatic Criticism*. Lawrence: University of Kansas Press, 1967. A study of Shaw's role in English drama during the 1890s when he was theater critic for the *Saturday Review*.

Gibbs, A. M. *Shaw*. Edinburgh: Oliver & Boyd, 1969. Volume on Shaw in the "Writers and Critics" series.

————. *The Art and Mind of Shaw: Essays in Criticism*. London: Macmillan, 1983. Explores connections between Shaw's intellectual preoccupations and the artistry of the plays.

Gordon, David J. *Bernard Shaw and the Comic Sublime*. London: Macmillan, 1990. Discusses Shaw as a "dramatic poet" with a focus on Shavian versions of sublimity.

Grene, Nicholas. *Bernard Shaw: A Critical View*. London: Macmillan, 1984. A challenging, often adversely critical, study of the plays.

Kaufmann, R. J., ed. *G. B. Shaw: A Collection of Critical Essays*. Englewood Cliffs, N.J.: Prentice-Hall, 1965. Volume on Shaw in the "Twentieth-Century Views" series.

Kronenberger, Louis, ed. *George Bernard Shaw: A Critical Survey*. Cleveland and New York: World Publishing Co., 1953. Collects some important early essays on Shaw.

MacCarthy, Desmond. *Shaw*. London: MacGibbon and Kee, 1951. A collection of MacCarthy's essays, reviews, and other writings on Shaw from 1907 to 1950.

Morgan, Margery M. *The Shavian Playground: An Exploration of the Art of George Bernard Shaw*. London: Methuen, 1972. A critical study of Shaw's dramatic artistry and the intellectual and literary affiliations of the plays.

————. *Bernard Shaw*. 2 vols. Windsor, Berkshire, U.K.: Profile Books, 1982. In the "Writers and Their Work" series.

Meisel, Martin. *Shaw and the Nineteenth-Century Theater*. Princeton, N.J.: Princeton University Press, 1963. Study of Shaw's knowledge and use of nineteenth-century theatrical conventions.

Ohmann, Richard M. *Shaw: The Style and the Man*. Middletown, Conn.:

Wesleyan University Press, 1962. Applies theories and techniques of stylistics to an analysis of Shaw's writings.

Peters, Margot. *Mrs. Pat: The Life of Mrs. Patrick Campbell*. London: Hamish Hamilton, 1985. Biography of the "perilously bewitching" actress.

Turco, Alfred. *Shaw's Moral Vision: The Self and Salvation*. Ithaca, N.Y.: Cornell University Press, 1976. Traces the development of Shaw's moral and philosophic vision in nondramatic and dramatic writings.

Valency, Maurice J. *The Cart and the Trumpet: The Plays of George Bernard Shaw*. New York: Oxford University Press, 1973. A study of Shaw's work in relation to the artistic, social, intellectual, and theatrical currents of his time.

Weintraub, Rodelle, ed. *Fabian Feminist: Bernard Shaw and Woman*. University Park and London: Pennsylvania State University Press, 1977. A collection of essays on Shaw's attitudes toward women, with several of his own speeches and writings on feminist issues.

Whitman, R. F. *Shaw and the Play of Ideas*. Ithaca, N.Y.: Cornell University Press, 1977. An exposition of Shaw's philosophical ideas and study of their treatment in the plays.

Wilson, Edmund. *The Triple Thinkers*. Harmondsworth: Penguin, 1962. Contains Wilson's influential general essay "Bernard Shaw at Eighty."

Wisenthal, J. L. *The Marriage of Contraries: Bernard Shaw's Middle Plays*. Cambridge: Harvard University Press, 1974. Study of Shaw's middle plays referring to Blakean concepts of contrariety.

____. *Shaw's Sense of History*. Oxford: Clarendon Press, 1988. A study of Shaw's attitudes toward history and dramatic uses of historical material.

Wright, Anne. *Literature of Crisis, 1910–1922: Howards End, Heartbreak House, Women in Love and The Waste Land*. London: Methuen, 1984. Includes a study of *Heartbreak House* in relation to other literary responses to the crisis period of the title.

Bibliographies/Reference

Laurence, Dan H. *Bernard Shaw: A Bibliography*. 2 vols. Oxford: Oxford University Press, 1983.

Morgan, Margery M. *File on Shaw*. London: Methuen, 1989. Contains extracts from early reviews of the plays, and other useful information.

Shaw: An Annotated Bibliography of Writings about Him. 3 vols. Volume 1 edited by J. P. Wearing; volume 2 edited by Elsie B. Adams and Donald C. Haberman; volume 3 edited by Donald C. Haberman. DeKalb: Northern Illinois University Press, 1986–87.

Selected Bibliography

Shaw Periodicals

Annual of Shaw Studies (formerly the *Shaw Review*). Includes regular bibliographical checklist.

Independent Shavian

Shavian

Articles on *Heartbreak House*

Coleman, D. C. "Fun and Games: Two Pictures of *Heartbreak House.*" *Drama
Survey* 5, no. 1 (Spring 1966): 223–36.

Corrigan, Robert W. "*Heartbreak House*: Shaw's Elegy for Europe." *Shaw
Review* 2, pt. 9 (1959): 2–6.

Garner, Stanton B., Jr. "Shaw's Comedy of Disillusionment." *Modern Drama*
28, no. 4 (December 1985): 638–58.

Gibbs, A. M. "Bernard Shaw's Other Island." In *Irish Culture and
Nationalism, 1750–1950*, edited by Oliver MacDonagh, W. F. Mandle,
and Pauric Travers, 122–36. London and Basingstoke: Macmillan,
1983.

Hornby, Richard. "The Symbolic Action of *Heartbreak House.*" *Drama Survey*
7 (1968–69): 5–24.

Hoy, Cyrus. "Shaw's Tragicomic Irony: From *Man and Superman* to
Heartbreak House." *Virginia Quarterly Review* 47 (1971): 57–78.

Kaufman, Michael W. "The Dissonance of Dialectic: Shaw's *Heartbreak
House.*" *Shaw Review* 13, no. 1 (January 1970): 2–9.

Kruse, Axel. "Bernard Shaw's *Heartbreak House*: The War in 'Neverland.'"
Sydney Studies in English 13 (1987–88): 100–19.

Leary, D. J. "Shaw's Blakean Vision: A Dialectic Approach to *Heartbreak
House.*" *Modern Drama* 15, no. 1 (May 1972): 89–103.

McDowell, Frederick P. W. "Technique, Symbol and Theme in *Heartbreak
House.*" *PMLA* 68, no. 3 (1953): 335–56.

____. "Apocalypse and After: Recent Interpretations of *Heartbreak House.*"
Independent Shavian 25, nos. 1–2 (1987): 3–15.

Meisel, Martin. "Shaw and Revolution." In *Shaw: Seven Critical Essays*, edited
by Norman Rosenblood, 107–34. Toronto: University of Toronto Press,
1971.

Nathan, Rhoda B. "The 'Daimons' of *Heartbreak House.*" *Modern Drama* 21
(1978): 253–65.

____. "The House with No Exit: The Existential Shaw." *Independent Shavian*
25, no. 3 (1987): 35–42.

Nethercot, Arthur H. "Zeppelins over *Heartbreak House*." *Shaw Review* 9, no. 2 (1966): 46–51.

Quinn, Martin. "The Dickensian Presence in *Heartbreak House*." *Shaw Review* 20, no. 3 (1977): 119–25.

Stockholder, Fred E. "A Schopenhauerian Reading of *Heartbreak House*." *Shaw Review* 19 (1976): 22–43.

Thaler, Estelle Manette. "Apocalyptic Vision in *Heartbreak House* and *Endgame*: The Metaphor of Change." *Zeitschrift fur Anglistik und Amerikanistik* 24, no. 4 (1986): 343–51.

Throne, Marilyn. "Madness, Mysticism, and Black Cultures: G. B. Shaw's Peter Keegan and Captain Shotover." *Colby Library Quarterly* 23, no. 3 (September 1987): 123–34.

Ure, Peter. "Master and Pupil in Bernard Shaw." *Essays in Criticism* 19, no. 2 (April 1969): 118–39.

Vogt, Sally Peters. "*Heartbreak House*: Shaw's Ship of Fools." *Modern Drama* 21 (1978): 267–86.

Wilkenfeld, Roger B. "Perpetual Motion in *Heartbreak House*." *Texas Studies in Literature and Language* 13, no. 1 (Spring 1971): 321–35.

Woodfield, James. "Ellie in Wonderland: Dream and Madness in *Heartbreak House*." *Englishj140*

Studies in Canada 11, no. 3 (September 1985): 334–45.

Index

Adams, Elsie B.: *Bernard Shaw and the Aesthetes*, 20; "Feminism and Female Stereotypes in Shaw," 128n9
Agate, James, 17
Alice in Wonderland, 131n2, 132n5
Altizer, Thomas: *History as Apocalypse*, 89
apocalypse, 8, 23, 44, 46, 53, 56, 67, 81–82, 86–94,102–110, 113, 133n5, 134n16, 134n17
Archer, William, 5
Ashwell, Lena, 10
Auerbach, Nina: *Woman and the Demon*, 33
Austen, Jane: *Persuasion*, 42

Barker, Harley Granville, 29
Barrie, James M.: *Peter Pan*, 31
Bentley, Eric: *Bernard Shaw*, 7, 18–19
Bernard Shaw: Collected Letters (ed. Dan H. Laurence), 8–9, 10–11, 27, 29, 34, 38, 39, 95, 105, 129n11
Bernard Shaw and Mrs. Patrick Campbell: Their Correspondence (ed. Alan Dent), 29, 30–31, 32, 33, 37, 125n5
Berst, Charles A.: *Bernard Shaw and the Art of Drama*, 20
Bertolini, John: *The Playwrighting Self of Bernard Shaw*, 129n16
Besant, Annie, 77–79
Bible, The: *Book of Daniel, The*, 87; *Gospel According to St. Matthew*, 88, 108; *Revelation of St. John the Divine, The*, 87, 88, 90, 104, 108, 135n27
Biblical apocalyptists, 87–88, 104–106
Blake, William: *Marriage of Heaven and Hell, The*, 89, 133n5
Blavatsky, Madame Helena Petrovna: *Secret Doctrine, The*, 79–80, 132n2, 132n3

Index

The Author

A.M. Gibbs is a Professor of English at Macquarie University, Sydney, Australia, and a Fellow of the Australian Academy of the Humanities. After graduating from the Universities of Melbourne and Oxford, he held posts in several British and Australian universities before taking up his present appointment in 1975. His research and teaching interests are in the fields of Renaissance literature and nineteenth century British, Irish, Scandinavian and European literature and drama. Amongst his previous publications are four books on various aspects of the life and work of Bernard Shaw, including *The Art and Mind of Shaw: Essays in Criticism* (1983) and *Shaw: Interviews and Recollections* (1990). He is currently producing an electronic research database on Shaw, and writing a literary file of the playwright.